MW00825047

Cram101 Textbook Outlines to accompany:

Microbiology : An Introduction

Gerard J. Tortora, 10th Edition

A Cram101 Inc. publication (c) 2010.

Cram101 Textbook Outlines and Cram101.com are Cram101 Inc. publications and services. All notes, highlights, reviews, and practice tests are written and prepared by Cram101, all rights reserved.

PRACTICE EXAMS.

Get all of the self-teaching practice exams for each chapter of this textbook at **www.Cram101.com** and ace the tests. Here is an example:

Chapter 1

Microbiology : An Introduction
Gerard J. Tortora, 10th Edition,
All Material Written and Prepared by Cram101

I WANT A BETTER GRADE.

1 _____ is a genus of gamma proteobacteria, belonging to the larger family of pseudomonads.

Recently, 16S rRNA sequence analysis has redefined the taxonomy of many bacterial species. As a result the genus _____ includes strains formerly classified in the genera Chryseomonas and Flavimonas.

○ Pseudomonas ○ P008
○ P1-derived artificial chromosome ○ P22

2 _____ played a major role during the Civil War. _____ not only preserved food in the days before refrigeration, but was also vital in the curing of leather. Union general William Tecumseh Sherman once said that "_____ is eminently contraband", as an army that has _____ can adequately feed its men.

○ Salt ○ Saccharomyces
○ Saccharomyces cerevisiae ○ Saccharophagus degradans

3 _____ is a genus of Gram-positive bacteria. Under the microscope they appear round , and form in grape-like clusters.

The _____ genus include just thirty-three species.

○ Staphylococcus ○ Saccharomyces
○ Saccharomyces cerevisiae ○ Saccharophagus degradans

4 _____ is the most common cause of staph infections. It is a spherical bacterium, frequently part of the skin

You get a 50% discount for the online exams. Go to **Cram101.com**, click Sign Up at the top of the screen, and enter DK73DW8421 in the promo code box on the registration screen. Access to Cram101.com is $4.95 per month, cancel at any time.

With Cram101.com online, you also have access to extensive reference material.

You will nail those essays and papers. Here is an example from a Cram101 Biology text:

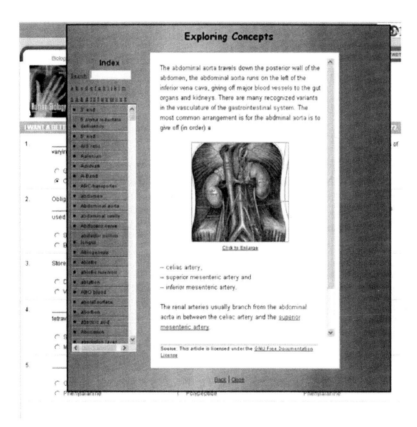

Visit **www.Cram101.com**, click Sign Up at the top of the screen, and enter DK73DW8421 in the promo code box on the registration screen. Access to www.Cram101.com is normally $9.95 per month, but because you have purchased this book, your access fee is only $4.95 per month, cancel at any time. Sign up and stop highlighting textbooks forever.

Learning System

Cram101 Textbook Outlines is a learning system. The notes in this book are the highlights of your textbook, you will never have to highlight a book again.

How to use this book. Take this book to class, it is your notebook for the lecture. The notes and highlights on the left hand side of the pages follow the outline and order of the textbook. All you have to do is follow along while your instructor presents the lecture. Circle the items emphasized in class and add other important information on the right side. With Cram101 Textbook Outlines you'll spend less time writing and more time listening. Learning becomes more efficient.

Cram101.com Online

Increase your studying efficiency by using Cram101.com's practice tests and online reference material. It is the perfect complement to Cram101 Textbook Outlines. Use self-teaching matching tests or simulate in-class testing with comprehensive multiple choice tests, or simply use Cram's true and false tests for quick review. Cram101.com even allows you to enter your in-class notes for an integrated studying format combining the textbook notes with your class notes.

Visit **www.Cram101.com**, click Sign Up at the top of the screen, and enter **DK73DW8421** in the promo code box on the registration screen. Access to www.Cram101.com is normally $9.95 per month, but because you have purchased this book, your access fee is only $4.95 per month. Sign up and stop highlighting textbooks forever.

Copyright © 2010 by Cram101, Inc. All rights reserved. "Cram101"® and "Never Highlight a Book Again!"® are registered trademarks of Cram101, Inc. ISBN(s): 9781616542665. EDE-3 .20091229

Microbiology : An Introduction
Gerard J. Tortora, 10th

CONTENTS

Chapter 1. The Microbial World and You

Pseudomonas	Pseudomonas is a genus of gamma proteobacteria, belonging to the larger family of pseudomonads. Recently, 16S rRNA sequence analysis has redefined the taxonomy of many bacterial species. As a result the genus Pseudomonas includes strains formerly classified in the genera Chryseomonas and Flavimonas.
Salt	Salt played a major role during the Civil War. Salt not only preserved food in the days before refrigeration, but was also vital in the curing of leather. Union general William Tecumseh Sherman once said that "Salt is eminently contraband", as an army that has Salt can adequately feed its men.
Staphylococcus	Staphylococcus is a genus of Gram-positive bacteria. Under the microscope they appear round , and form in grape-like clusters. The Staphylococcus genus include just thirty-three species.
Staphylococcus aureus	Staphylococcus aureus is the most common cause of staph infections. It is a spherical bacterium, frequently part of the skin flora found in the nose and on skin. About 20% of the population are long-term carriers of S. aureus.
Prochlorococcus	Prochlorococcus is a genus of very small (0.6 µm) marine cyanobacteria with an unusual pigmentation (chlorophyll b) belonging to photosynthetic picoplankton. It is probably the most abundant photosynthetic organism on Earth. Although there had been several earlier records of very small chlorophyll-b-containing cyanobacteria in the ocean, Prochlorococcus was actually discovered in 1986 by Sallie W. (Penny) Chisholm of the Massachusetts Institute of Technology, Robert J. Olson of the Woods Hole Oceanographic Institution, and other collaborators in the Sargasso Sea using flow cytometry.
Salmonella	Salmonella is a genus of rod-shaped, Gram-negative, non-spore forming, predominantly motile enterobacteria with diameters around 0.7 to 1.5 µm, lengths from 2 to 5 µm, and flagella which project in all directions (i.e. peritrichous.) They are chemoorganotrophs, obtaining their energy from oxidation and reduction reactions using organic sources and are facultative anaerobes; most species produce hydrogen sulfide, which can readily be detected by growing them on media containing ferrous sulfate, such as TSI. Most isolates exist in two phases; phase I is the motile phase and phase II the non-motile phase. Cultures that are non-motile upon primary culture may be swithched to the motile phase using a Craigie tube.
Thermophile	A Thermophile is an organism -- a type of extremophile -- that thrives at relatively high temperatures, between 45 and 80 °C (113 and 176 °F.) Many Thermophile s are archaea. Thermophile s are found in various geothermally heated regions of the Earth such as hot springs like those in Yellowstone National Park and deep sea hydrothermal vents, as well as decaying plant matter such as peat bogs and compost.
Paramyxovirus	Paramyxovirus es are viruses of the Paramyxoviridae family of the Mononegavirales order; they are negative-sense single-stranded RNA viruses responsible for a number of human and animal diseases. · Subfamily Paramyxovirinae

Go to **Cram101.com** for Interactive Practice Exams for this book or virtually any of your books for $4.95/month.
And, **NEVER** highlight a book again!

· Genus Avulavirus (type species Newcastle disease virus)

· Genus Henipavirus (type species Hendravirus; others include Nipahvirus)

· Genus Morbillivirus (type species Measles virus; others include Rinderpest virus, Canine distemper virus, phocine distemper virus, Peste des Petits Ruminants virus (PPR))

· Genus Respirovirus (type species Sendai virus; others include Human parainfluenza viruses 1 and 3, as well some of the viruses of the common cold)

· Genus Rubulavirus (type species Mumps virus; others include Human parainfluenza viruses 2 and 4, Simian parainfluenza virus 5, Menangle virus, Tioman virus)

· Genus TPMV-like viruses (type species Tupaia Paramyxovirus

· Subfamily Pneumovirinae

· Genus Pneumovirus (type species Human respiratory syncytial virus, others include Bovine respiratory syncytial virus)

· Genus Metapneumovirus (type species Avian pneumovirus, Human metapneumovirus)

· Unassigned viruses

· Fer-de-Lance virus

· Nariva virus

· Tupaia Paramyxovirus

· Salem virus

· J virus

· Mossman virus

· Beilong virus

Virions are enveloped and can be spherical, filamentous or pleomorphic. Fusion proteins and attachment proteins appear as spikes on the virion surface. Matrix proteins inside the envelope stabilise virus structure.

Veillonella	Veillonella are gram-negative anaerobic cocci. This bacterium is well known for its lactate fermenting abilities. They are a normal bacterium in the intestines and oral mucosa of mammals.
Tuberculosis	Tuberculosis is a common and often deadly infectious disease caused by mycobacteria, in humans mainly Mycobacterium Tuberculosis . Tuberculosis usually attacks the lungs (as pulmonary TB) but can also affect the central nervous system, the lymphatic system, the circulatory system, the genitourinary system, the gastrointestinal system, bones, joints, and even the skin. Other mycobacteria such as Mycobacterium bovis, Mycobacterium africanum, Mycobacterium canetti, and Mycobacterium microti also cause Tuberculosis, but these species are less common in humans.
Bacillus stearothermophilus	Bacillus stearothermophilus (or GeoBacillus stearothermophilus) is a rod-shaped, Gram-positive bacterium and a member of the division Firmicutes. The bacteria is a thermophile and is widely distributed in soil, hot springs, ocean sediment, and is a cause of spoilage in food products. It will grow within a temperature range of 30-75 degrees celsius.

Go to **Cram101.com** for Interactive Practice Exams for this book or virtually any of your books for $4.95/month.
And, **NEVER** highlight a book again!

Bacillus anthracis	Bacillus anthracis is a Gram-positive spore-forming, rod-shaped bacterium, with a width of 1-1.2Âμm and a length of 3-5Âμm. It can be grown in an ordinary nutrient medium under aerobic or anaerobic conditions. It is the only bacterium with a protein capsule (D-glutamate), and the only pathogenic bacteria to carry its own adenylyl cyclase virulence factor (edema factor).
Shigella	Shigella is a genus of Gram-negative, non-spore forming rod-shaped bacteria closely related to Escherichia coli and Salmonella. The causative agent of human shigellosis, Shigella cause disease in primates, but not in other mammals. It is only naturally found in humans and apes.
Neisseria	The Neisseria are a large family of commensal bacteria that colonize the mucosal surfaces of many animals. Of the eleven species that colonize humans, only two are pathogens. N. meningitidis and N. gonorrhoeae often cause asymptomatic infections, a commensal-like behavior.
Neisseria gonorrhoeae	Neisseria gonorrhoeae or Gonococcus, is a species of Gram-negative kidney bean-shaped diplococci bacteria responsible for the sexually transmitted disease gonorrhoea. N.gonorrhoeae was first described by Albert Neisser in 1879. Neisseria are fastidious cocci, requiring nutrient supplementation to grow in laboratory cultures.
Sulfolobus	In taxonomy, Sulfolobus is a genus of the Sulfolobaceae. Sulfolobus species grow in volcanic springs with optimal growth occurring at pH 2-3 and temperatures of 75-80 °C, making them acidophiles and thermophiles respectively. Sulfolobus cells are irregularly shaped and flagellar.
Syphilis	Syphilis is a sexually transmitted disease caused by the spirochetal bacterium Treponema pallidum subspecies pallidum. The route of transmission of Syphilis is almost always through sexual contact, although there are examples of congenital Syphilis via transmission from mother to child in utero. The signs and symptoms of Syphilis are numerous; before the advent of serological testing, precise diagnosis was very difficult.
Vancomycin-resistant	Vancomycin-resistant enterococcus (VRE) is the name given to a group of bacterial species of the genus Enterococcus that is resistant to the antibiotic vancomycin. Enterococci are enteric and can be found in the digestive and urinary tracts of some humans. VRE was discovered in 1985 and is particularly dangerous to immunocompromised individuals.
Vancomycin-resistant Staphylococcus aureus	Vancomycin-resistant Staphylococcus aureus is a strain of Staphylococcus aureus that has become resistant to the glycopeptide antibiotic vancomycin. With the increase of staphylococcal resistance to methicillin, vancomycin (or another antibiotic teicoplanin) is often a treatment of choice in infections with methicillin-resistant Staphylococcus aureus (MRSA.) Vancomycin resistance is still a rare occurrence.
Thiomargarita namibiensis	Thiomargarita namibiensis is a gram-negative coccoid Proteobacterium, found in the ocean sediments of the continental shelf of Namibia. It is the largest bacterium ever discovered, generally 0.1 - 0.3 mm (100 - 300 Âμm) wide, but sometimes up to 0.75 mm (750 Âμm.)

Go to **Cram101.com** for Interactive Practice Exams for this book or virtually any of your books for $4.95/month.
And, **NEVER** highlight a book again!

	The genus name is formed from Greek θειον = sulfur , and Latin margarita = pearl.
Pertussis	Pertussis is a highly contagious disease caused by the bacterium Bordetella Pertussis It derived its name from the "whoop" sound made from the inspiration of air after a cough. A similar, milder disease is caused by B. para Pertussis .
Tetanus	Tetanus is a medical condition characterized by a prolonged contraction of skeletal muscle fibers. The primary symptoms are caused by tetanospasmin, a neurotoxin produced by the Gram-positive, obligate anaerobic bacterium Clostridium tetani. Infection generally occurs through wound contamination and often involves a cut or deep puncture wound.
Neisseria meningitidis	Neisseria meningitidis is a heterotrophic gram-negative diplococcal bacterium best known for its role in meningitis and other forms of meningococcal disease such as meningococcemia. N. meningitidis is a major cause of morbidity and mortality in childhood in industrialized countries and is responsible for epidemics in Africa and in Asia. Approximately 2500 to 3500 cases of N meningitidis infection occur annually in the United States, with a case rate of about 1 in 100,000.
RecA	RecA is a 38 kilodalton Escherichia coli protein essential for the repair and maintenance of DNA. RecA has a structural and functional homolog in every species in which it has been seriously sought and serves as an archetype for this class of homologous DNA repair proteins. The homologous protein in Homo sapiens is called RAD51. RecA has multiple activities, all related to DNA repair.
Streptobacillus	Streptobacillus is a genus of aerobic, gram-negative facultative anaerobe bacteria, which grow in culture as rods in chains. Species associated with infection - S. moniliformis Reported susceptibilities and therapies - penicillin, erythromycin Associated infections: the Haverhill fever form of rat bite fever. (Notes Spirillum minus is also an agent of rat bite fever, in the form known as sodoku.)
Virology	In virology, temperate refers to the ability of some bacteriophages (notable coliphage λ) to display a lysogenic life cycle. Many (but not all) temperate phages can integrate their genomes into their host bacterium"s chromosome, together becoming a lysogen as the phage genome becomes a prophage. A temperate phage is also able to undergo a productive, typically lytic life cycle, where the prophage is expressed, replicates the phage genome, and produces phage progeny, which then leave the bacterium.
Rhizobium	Rhizobium is a genus of Gram-negative soil bacteria that fix nitrogen. Rhizobium forms an endosymbiotic nitrogen fixing association with roots of legumes. The bacteria colonize plant cells within root nodules.

Go to **Cram101.com** for Interactive Practice Exams for this book or virtually any of your books for $4.95/month.
And, **NEVER** highlight a book again!

Pasteurella	Pasteurella is a genus of Gram-negative, facultatively anaerobic bacteria. Pasturella species are non-motile and pleomorphic. Most species are catalase- and oxidase-positive.
Salmonella enterica	Salmonella enterica is a rod shaped, flagellated, aerobic, Gram-negative bacterium, and a member of the genus Salmonella. S. enterica has an extraordinarily large number of serovars or strains--up to 2000 have been described. · Salmonella enterica Serovar Typhi (historically elevated to species status as S. typhi) is the disease agent in typhoid fever. The genome sequences of Serovar Typhi has been established. · Salmonella enterica Serovar Typhimurium (also known as S. typhimurium) can lead to a form of human gastroenteritis sometimes referred to as salmonellosis. · The genome sequences of serovar Typhimurium LT2 have been established. Also an analysis of the proteome of Typhimurium LT2 under differing environmental conditions has been performed .
Necrotizing fasciitis	Necrotizing fasciitis , commonly known as flesh-eating disease or flesh-eating bacteria, is a rare infection of the deeper layers of skin and subcutaneous tissues, easily spreading across the fascial plane within the subcutaneous tissue. Type I describes a polymicrobial infection, whereas Type II describes a monomicrobial infection. Many types of bacteria can cause Necrotizing fasciitis (eg.

Go to **Cram101.com** for Interactive Practice Exams for this book or virtually any of your books for $4.95/month.
And, **NEVER** highlight a book again!

Salmonella	Salmonella is a genus of rod-shaped, Gram-negative, non-spore forming, predominantly motile enterobacteria with diameters around 0.7 to 1.5 µm, lengths from 2 to 5 µm, and flagella which project in all directions (i.e. peritrichous.) They are chemoorganotrophs, obtaining their energy from oxidation and reduction reactions using organic sources and are facultative anaerobes; most species produce hydrogen sulfide, which can readily be detected by growing them on media containing ferrous sulfate, such as TSI. Most isolates exist in two phases; phase I is the motile phase and phase II the non-motile phase. Cultures that are non-motile upon primary culture may be swithched to the motile phase using a Craigie tube.
Staphylococcus	Staphylococcus is a genus of Gram-positive bacteria. Under the microscope they appear round , and form in grape-like clusters. The Staphylococcus genus include just thirty-three species.
Staphylococcus aureus	Staphylococcus aureus is the most common cause of staph infections. It is a spherical bacterium, frequently part of the skin flora found in the nose and on skin. About 20% of the population are long-term carriers of S. aureus.
Salt	Salt played a major role during the Civil War. Salt not only preserved food in the days before refrigeration, but was also vital in the curing of leather. Union general William Tecumseh Sherman once said that "Salt is eminently contraband", as an army that has Salt can adequately feed its men.
Prochlorococcus	Prochlorococcus is a genus of very small (0.6 µm) marine cyanobacteria with an unusual pigmentation (chlorophyll b) belonging to photosynthetic picoplankton. It is probably the most abundant photosynthetic organism on Earth. Although there had been several earlier records of very small chlorophyll-b-containing cyanobacteria in the ocean, Prochlorococcus was actually discovered in 1986 by Sallie W. (Penny) Chisholm of the Massachusetts Institute of Technology, Robert J. Olson of the Woods Hole Oceanographic Institution, and other collaborators in the Sargasso Sea using flow cytometry.
Thermotoga	Thermotoga are thermophile or hyperthermophile bacteria whose cell is wrapped in an outer "toga" membrane. They were named by microbiologist Karl Stetter. They metabolize carbohydrates.
Yersinia	Yersinia is a genus of bacteria in the family Enterobacteriaceae. Yersinia are Gram-negative rod shaped bacteria, a few micrometers long and fractions of a micrometer in diameter, and are facultative anaerobes. Some members of Yersinia are pathogenic in humans.
Pseudomonas	Pseudomonas is a genus of gamma proteobacteria, belonging to the larger family of pseudomonads. Recently, 16S rRNA sequence analysis has redefined the taxonomy of many bacterial species. As a result the genus Pseudomonas includes strains formerly classified in the genera Chryseomonas and Flavimonas.
RecA	RecA is a 38 kilodalton Escherichia coli protein essential for the repair and maintenance of DNA. RecA has a structural and functional homolog in every species in which it has been seriously sought and serves as an archetype for this class of homologous DNA repair proteins. The homologous protein in Homo sapiens is called RAD51.

Go to **Cram101.com** for Interactive Practice Exams for this book or virtually any of your books for $4.95/month.
And, **NEVER** highlight a book again!

	RecA has multiple activities, all related to DNA repair.
Sulfolobus	In taxonomy, Sulfolobus is a genus of the Sulfolobaceae.
	Sulfolobus species grow in volcanic springs with optimal growth occurring at pH 2-3 and temperatures of 75-80 °C, making them acidophiles and thermophiles respectively. Sulfolobus cells are irregularly shaped and flagellar.
Sulfate-reducing bacteria	Sulfate-reducing bacteria comprise several groups of bacteria that use sulfate as an oxidizing agent, reducing it to sulfide. Most Sulfate-reducing bacteria can also use other oxidized sulfur compounds such as sulfite and thiosulfate, or elemental sulfur. This type of metabolism is called dissimilatory, since sulfur is not incorporated - assimilated - into any organic compounds.
Shigella	Shigella is a genus of Gram-negative, non-spore forming rod-shaped bacteria closely related to Escherichia coli and Salmonella. The causative agent of human shigellosis, Shigella cause disease in primates, but not in other mammals. It is only naturally found in humans and apes.
Neisseria	The Neisseria are a large family of commensal bacteria that colonize the mucosal surfaces of many animals. Of the eleven species that colonize humans, only two are pathogens. N. meningitidis and N. gonorrhoeae often cause asymptomatic infections, a commensal-like behavior.
Neisseria gonorrhoeae	Neisseria gonorrhoeae or Gonococcus, is a species of Gram-negative kidney bean-shaped diplococci bacteria responsible for the sexually transmitted disease gonorrhoea.
	N.gonorrhoeae was first described by Albert Neisser in 1879.
	Neisseria are fastidious cocci, requiring nutrient supplementation to grow in laboratory cultures.
Vibrio	Vibrio is a genus of Gram-negative bacteria possessing a curved rod shape. Typically found in saltwater, Vibrio are facultative anaerobes that test positive for oxidase and do not form spores. All members of the genus are motile and have polar flagella with sheaths.
Vibrio cholerae	Vibrio cholerae is a motile gram negative curved-rod shaped bacterium with a polar flagellum that causes cholera in humans. V. cholerae and other species of the genus Vibrio belong to the gamma subdivision of the Proteobacteria.
	There are two major strains of V. cholerae, classic and El Tor, and numerous other serogroups.
Tuberculosis	Tuberculosis is a common and often deadly infectious disease caused by mycobacteria, in humans mainly Mycobacterium Tuberculosis . Tuberculosis usually attacks the lungs (as pulmonary TB) but can also affect the central nervous system, the lymphatic system, the circulatory system, the genitourinary system, the gastrointestinal system, bones, joints, and even the skin. Other mycobacteria such as Mycobacterium bovis, Mycobacterium africanum, Mycobacterium canetti, and Mycobacterium microti also cause Tuberculosis, but these species are less common in humans.

Go to **Cram101.com** for Interactive Practice Exams for this book or virtually any of your books for $4.95/month.
And, **NEVER** highlight a book again!

Rocky Mountain spotted fever	Rocky Mountain spotted fever is the most lethal and most frequently reported rickettsial illness in the United States. It has been diagnosed throughout the Americas. Some synonyms for Rocky Mountain spotted fever in other countries include "tick typhus," "Tobia fever" (Colombia), "São Paulo fever" or "febre maculosa" (Brazil), and "fiebre manchada" (Mexico.)
Prevotella	Prevotella is a genus of bacteria. "Bacteroides melaninogenicus" has recently been reclassified and split into Prevotella melaninogenica and Prevotella intermedia. Several species have been implicated in oral disease.
Neisseria meningitidis	Neisseria meningitidis is a heterotrophic gram-negative diplococcal bacterium best known for its role in meningitis and other forms of meningococcal disease such as meningococcemia. N. meningitidis is a major cause of morbidity and mortality in childhood in industrialized countries and is responsible for epidemics in Africa and in Asia. Approximately 2500 to 3500 cases of N meningitidis infection occur annually in the United States, with a case rate of about 1 in 100,000.
Syphilis	Syphilis is a sexually transmitted disease caused by the spirochetal bacterium Treponema pallidum subspecies pallidum. The route of transmission of Syphilis is almost always through sexual contact, although there are examples of congenital Syphilis via transmission from mother to child in utero. The signs and symptoms of Syphilis are numerous; before the advent of serological testing, precise diagnosis was very difficult.

Go to **Cram101.com** for Interactive Practice Exams for this book or virtually any of your books for $4.95/month.
And, **NEVER** highlight a book again!

Micrococcus	Micrococcus (mi" krÅ kÅ k" Æ s) is a genus of bacteria in the Micrococcaceae family. Micrococcus occurs in a wide range of environments, including water, dust, and soil. Micrococci have Gram-positive spherical cells ranging from about 0.5 to 3 micrometers in diameter and are typically appear in tetrads.
Bacillus anthracis	Bacillus anthracis is a Gram-positive spore-forming, rod-shaped bacterium, with a width of 1-1.2Âµm and a length of 3-5Âµm. It can be grown in an ordinary nutrient medium under aerobic or anaerobic conditions. It is the only bacterium with a protein capsule (D-glutamate), and the only pathogenic bacteria to carry its own adenylyl cyclase virulence factor (edema factor).
Tuberculosis	Tuberculosis is a common and often deadly infectious disease caused by mycobacteria, in humans mainly Mycobacterium Tuberculosis . Tuberculosis usually attacks the lungs (as pulmonary TB) but can also affect the central nervous system, the lymphatic system, the circulatory system, the genitourinary system, the gastrointestinal system, bones, joints, and even the skin. Other mycobacteria such as Mycobacterium bovis, Mycobacterium africanum, Mycobacterium canetti, and Mycobacterium microti also cause Tuberculosis, but these species are less common in humans.
Pseudomonas	Pseudomonas is a genus of gamma proteobacteria, belonging to the larger family of pseudomonads. Recently, 16S rRNA sequence analysis has redefined the taxonomy of many bacterial species. As a result the genus Pseudomonas includes strains formerly classified in the genera Chryseomonas and Flavimonas.
RecA	RecA is a 38 kilodalton Escherichia coli protein essential for the repair and maintenance of DNA. RecA has a structural and functional homolog in every species in which it has been seriously sought and serves as an archetype for this class of homologous DNA repair proteins. The homologous protein in Homo sapiens is called RAD51. RecA has multiple activities, all related to DNA repair.
Erythromycin	Erythromycin is a macrolide antibiotic that has an antimicrobial spectrum similar to or slightly wider than that of penicillin, and is often used for people who have an allergy to penicillins. For respiratory tract infections, it has better coverage of atypical organisms, including mycoplasma and Legionellosis. It was first marketed by Eli Lilly and Company, and it is today commonly known as EES (Erythromycin ethylsuccinate, an ester prodrug that is commonly administered).
Prevotella	Prevotella is a genus of bacteria. "Bacteroides melaninogenicus" has recently been reclassified and split into Prevotella melaninogenica and Prevotella intermedia. Several species have been implicated in oral disease.
Shigella	Shigella is a genus of Gram-negative, non-spore forming rod-shaped bacteria closely related to Escherichia coli and Salmonella. The causative agent of human shigellosis, Shigella cause disease in primates, but not in other mammals. It is only naturally found in humans and apes.

Go to **Cram101.com** for Interactive Practice Exams for this book or virtually any of your books for $4.95/month.
And, **NEVER** highlight a book again!

Neisseria	The Neisseria are a large family of commensal bacteria that colonize the mucosal surfaces of many animals. Of the eleven species that colonize humans, only two are pathogens. N. meningitidis and N. gonorrhoeae often cause asymptomatic infections, a commensal-like behavior.
Neisseria gonorrhoeae	Neisseria gonorrhoeae or Gonococcus, is a species of Gram-negative kidney bean-shaped diplococci bacteria responsible for the sexually transmitted disease gonorrhoea.
	N.gonorrhoeae was first described by Albert Neisser in 1879.
	Neisseria are fastidious cocci, requiring nutrient supplementation to grow in laboratory cultures.
Spirillum	Spirillum in microbiology refers to a bacterium with a cell body that twists like a spiral. It is the third distinct bacterial cell shape type besides coccus and bacillus cells. Spirillum is a genus of gram-negative bacteria.

Go to **Cram101.com** for Interactive Practice Exams for this book or virtually any of your books for $4.95/month.
And, **NEVER** highlight a book again!

Neisseria	The Neisseria are a large family of commensal bacteria that colonize the mucosal surfaces of many animals. Of the eleven species that colonize humans, only two are pathogens. N. meningitidis and N. gonorrhoeae often cause asymptomatic infections, a commensal-like behavior.
Neisseria gonorrhoeae	Neisseria gonorrhoeae or Gonococcus, is a species of Gram-negative kidney bean-shaped diplococci bacteria responsible for the sexually transmitted disease gonorrhoea. N.gonorrhoeae was first described by Albert Neisser in 1879. Neisseria are fastidious cocci, requiring nutrient supplementation to grow in laboratory cultures.
Prochlorococcus	Prochlorococcus is a genus of very small (0.6 µm) marine cyanobacteria with an unusual pigmentation (chlorophyll b) belonging to photosynthetic picoplankton. It is probably the most abundant photosynthetic organism on Earth. Although there had been several earlier records of very small chlorophyll-b-containing cyanobacteria in the ocean, Prochlorococcus was actually discovered in 1986 by Sallie W. (Penny) Chisholm of the Massachusetts Institute of Technology, Robert J. Olson of the Woods Hole Oceanographic Institution, and other collaborators in the Sargasso Sea using flow cytometry.
Pseudomonas	Pseudomonas is a genus of gamma proteobacteria, belonging to the larger family of pseudomonads. Recently, 16S rRNA sequence analysis has redefined the taxonomy of many bacterial species. As a result the genus Pseudomonas includes strains formerly classified in the genera Chryseomonas and Flavimonas.
Streptobacillus	Streptobacillus is a genus of aerobic, gram-negative facultative anaerobe bacteria, which grow in culture as rods in chains. Species associated with infection - S. moniliformis Reported susceptibilities and therapies - penicillin, erythromycin Associated infections: the Haverhill fever form of rat bite fever. (Notes Spirillum minus is also an agent of rat bite fever, in the form known as sodoku.)
Rhizobium	Rhizobium is a genus of Gram-negative soil bacteria that fix nitrogen. Rhizobium forms an endosymbiotic nitrogen fixing association with roots of legumes. The bacteria colonize plant cells within root nodules.
Staphylococcus	Staphylococcus is a genus of Gram-positive bacteria. Under the microscope they appear round , and form in grape-like clusters. The Staphylococcus genus include just thirty-three species.
Bacillus anthracis	Bacillus anthracis is a Gram-positive spore-forming, rod-shaped bacterium, with a width of 1-1.2µm and a length of 3-5µm. It can be grown in an ordinary nutrient medium under aerobic or anaerobic conditions. It is the only bacterium with a protein capsule (D-glutamate), and the only pathogenic bacteria to carry its own adenylyl cyclase virulence factor (edema factor).

Go to **Cram101.com** for Interactive Practice Exams for this book or virtually any of your books for $4.95/month.
And, **NEVER** highlight a book again!

Klebsiella	Klebsiella is a genus of non-motile, Gram-negative, Oxidase-negative rod shaped bacteria with a prominent polysaccharide-based capsule. Frequent human pathogens, Klebsiella organisms can lead to a wide range of disease states, notably pneumonia, urinary tract infections, septicemia, ankylosing spondylitis, and soft tissue infections. Klebsiella species are ubiquitous in nature.
Slime layer	A Slime layer in bacteria is an easily removed, diffuse, unorganised layer of extracellular material that surrounds bacteria cells. Specifically, this consists mostly of exopolysaccharides, glycoproteins, and glycolipids. The Slime layer is not to be confused with the S-layer, a separate and highly organised glycoprotein layer surrounding many bacterial cells.
Proteus	Proteus is a genus of Gram-negative Proteobacteria. Three species--P. vulgaris, P. mirabilis, and P. penneri--are opportunistic human pathogens. Proteus includes pathogens responsible for many human urinary tract infections.
Spirillum	Spirillum in microbiology refers to a bacterium with a cell body that twists like a spiral. It is the third distinct bacterial cell shape type besides coccus and bacillus cells. Spirillum is a genus of gram-negative bacteria.
Staphylococcus aureus	Staphylococcus aureus is the most common cause of staph infections. It is a spherical bacterium, frequently part of the skin flora found in the nose and on skin. About 20% of the population are long-term carriers of S. aureus.
RecA	RecA is a 38 kilodalton Escherichia coli protein essential for the repair and maintenance of DNA. RecA has a structural and functional homolog in every species in which it has been seriously sought and serves as an archetype for this class of homologous DNA repair proteins. The homologous protein in Homo sapiens is called RAD51. RecA has multiple activities, all related to DNA repair.
Salmonella	Salmonella is a genus of rod-shaped, Gram-negative, non-spore forming, predominantly motile enterobacteria with diameters around 0.7 to 1.5 Âµm, lengths from 2 to 5 Âµm, and flagella which project in all directions (i.e. peritrichous.) They are chemoorganotrophs, obtaining their energy from oxidation and reduction reactions using organic sources and are facultative anaerobes; most species produce hydrogen sulfide, which can readily be detected by growing them on media containing ferrous sulfate, such as TSI. Most isolates exist in two phases; phase I is the motile phase and phase II the non-motile phase. Cultures that are non-motile upon primary culture may be swithched to the motile phase using a Craigie tube.
Shigella	Shigella is a genus of Gram-negative, non-spore forming rod-shaped bacteria closely related to Escherichia coli and Salmonella. The causative agent of human shigellosis, Shigella cause disease in primates, but not in other mammals. It is only naturally found in humans and apes.
Prevotella	Prevotella is a genus of bacteria.

Go to **Cram101.com** for Interactive Practice Exams for this book or virtually any of your books for $4.95/month.
And, **NEVER** highlight a book again!

	"Bacteroides melaninogenicus" has recently been reclassified and split into Prevotella melaninogenica and Prevotella intermedia. Several species have been implicated in oral disease.
Yersinia	Yersinia is a genus of bacteria in the family Enterobacteriaceae. Yersinia are Gram-negative rod shaped bacteria, a few micrometers long and fractions of a micrometer in diameter, and are facultative anaerobes. Some members of Yersinia are pathogenic in humans.
Erythromycin	Erythromycin is a macrolide antibiotic that has an antimicrobial spectrum similar to or slightly wider than that of penicillin, and is often used for people who have an allergy to penicillins. For respiratory tract infections, it has better coverage of atypical organisms, including mycoplasma and Legionellosis. It was first marketed by Eli Lilly and Company, and it is today commonly known as EES (Erythromycin ethylsuccinate, an ester prodrug that is commonly administered).
Salt	Salt played a major role during the Civil War. Salt not only preserved food in the days before refrigeration, but was also vital in the curing of leather. Union general William Tecumseh Sherman once said that "Salt is eminently contraband", as an army that has Salt can adequately feed its men.
Spheroplast	A Spheroplast is a cell from which the cell wall has been almost completely removed, as by the action of penicillin. The name stems from the fact that after a microbe"s cell wall is digested, membrane tension causes the cell to acquire a characteristic spherical shape. Spheroplast s are osmotically fragile, and will lyse if transferred to a hypotonic solution.
Vibrio	Vibrio is a genus of Gram-negative bacteria possessing a curved rod shape. Typically found in saltwater, Vibrio are facultative anaerobes that test positive for oxidase and do not form spores. All members of the genus are motile and have polar flagella with sheaths.
Vibrio cholerae	Vibrio cholerae is a motile gram negative curved-rod shaped bacterium with a polar flagellum that causes cholera in humans. V. cholerae and other species of the genus Vibrio belong to the gamma subdivision of the Proteobacteria. There are two major strains of V. cholerae, classic and El Tor, and numerous other serogroups.
Neisseria meningitidis	Neisseria meningitidis is a heterotrophic gram-negative diplococcal bacterium best known for its role in meningitis and other forms of meningococcal disease such as meningococcemia. N. meningitidis is a major cause of morbidity and mortality in childhood in industrialized countries and is responsible for epidemics in Africa and in Asia. Approximately 2500 to 3500 cases of N meningitidis infection occur annually in the United States, with a case rate of about 1 in 100,000.
Rhodospirillales	The Rhodospirillales are an order of proteobacteria, with two families. The Acetobacteraceae comprise the acetic acid bacteria, which are heterotrophic and produce acetic acid during their respiration. The Rhodospirillaceae include mainly purple non-sulfur bacteria, which produce energy through photosynthesis.

Go to **Cram101.com** for Interactive Practice Exams for this book or virtually any of your books for $4.95/month.
And, **NEVER** highlight a book again!

Rhodospirillum rubrum	Rhodospirillum rubrum is a Gram-negative, purple-coloured Proteobacterium, with a size of 800 to 1000 nanometers. As it can live both anaerobically (if cultured in an environment without light)and aerobically (if cultured in an environment with light), it is therefore both heterotrophic and autotrophic. Under aerobic growth photosynthesis is genetically suppressed and R. rubrum is then colorless.
Nucleoid	The Nucleoid is an irregularly-shaped region within the cell of prokaryotes which has nuclear material without a nuclear membrane and where the genetic material is localized. The genome of prokaryotic organisms generally is a circular, double-stranded piece of DNA, of which multiple copies may exist at any time. The length of a genome widely varies, but generally is at least a few million base pairs.
Serratia	Serratia is a genus of Gram-negative, facultatively anaerobic, rod-shaped bacteria of the Enterobacteriaceae family. The most common species in the genus, S. marcescens, is normally the only pathogen and usually causes nosocomial infections. However, rare strains of S. plymuthica, S. liquefaciens, S. rubidaea, and S. odoriferae have caused diseases through infection.
Serratia marcescens	Serratia marcescens is a species of Gram-negative, rod-shaped bacteria in the family Enterobacteriaceae. A human pathogen, S. marcescens is involved in nosocomial infections, particularly catheter-associated bacteremia, urinary tract infections and wound infections, and is responsible for 1.4% of nosocomial bacteremia cases in the United States. It is commonly found in the respiratory and urinary tracts of hospitalized adults and in the gastrointestinal system of children.
Thiomargarita namibiensis	Thiomargarita namibiensis is a gram-negative coccoid Proteobacterium, found in the ocean sediments of the continental shelf of Namibia. It is the largest bacterium ever discovered, generally 0.1 - 0.3 mm (100 - 300 µm) wide, but sometimes up to 0.75 mm (750 µm.) The genus name is formed from Greek θειον = sulfur , and Latin margarita = pearl.
Syphilis	Syphilis is a sexually transmitted disease caused by the spirochetal bacterium Treponema pallidum subspecies pallidum. The route of transmission of Syphilis is almost always through sexual contact, although there are examples of congenital Syphilis via transmission from mother to child in utero. The signs and symptoms of Syphilis are numerous; before the advent of serological testing, precise diagnosis was very difficult.
Q fever	Q fever is a disease caused by infection with Coxiella burnetii, a bacterium that affects both humans and animals. This organism is uncommon but may be found in cattle, sheep, goats and other domestic mammals, including cats and dogs. The infection results from inhalation of contaminated particles in the air, and from contact with the milk, urine, feces, vaginal mucus, or semen of infected animals.
Nitrifying bacteria	Nitrifying bacteria are chemoautotrophic bacteria that grow by consuming inorganic nitrogen compounds. Many species of Nitrifying bacteria have complex internal membrane systems that are the location for key enzymes in nitrification: ammonia monooxygenase which oxidizes ammonia to hydroxylamine, and nitrite oxidoreductase, which oxidizes nitrite to nitrate.

Go to **Cram101.com** for Interactive Practice Exams for this book or virtually any of your books for $4.95/month.
And, **NEVER** highlight a book again!

Nitrifying bacteria are widespread in soil and water, and are found in highest numbers where considerable amounts of ammonia are present (areas with extensive protein decomposition, and sewage treatment plants.)

Vancomycin-resistant

Vancomycin-resistant enterococcus (VRE) is the name given to a group of bacterial species of the genus Enterococcus that is resistant to the antibiotic vancomycin. Enterococci are enteric and can be found in the digestive and urinary tracts of some humans. VRE was discovered in 1985 and is particularly dangerous to immunocompromised individuals.

Micrococcus

Micrococcus (mi" krÅ kÅ k" Æ s) is a genus of bacteria in the Micrococcaceae family. Micrococcus occurs in a wide range of environments, including water, dust, and soil. Micrococci have Gram-positive spherical cells ranging from about 0.5 to 3 micrometers in diameter and are typically appear in tetrads.

Go to **Cram101.com** for Interactive Practice Exams for this book or virtually any of your books for $4.95/month.
And, **NEVER** highlight a book again!

Neisseria	The Neisseria are a large family of commensal bacteria that colonize the mucosal surfaces of many animals. Of the eleven species that colonize humans, only two are pathogens. N. meningitidis and N. gonorrhoeae often cause asymptomatic infections, a commensal-like behavior.
Neisseria meningitidis	Neisseria meningitidis is a heterotrophic gram-negative diplococcal bacterium best known for its role in meningitis and other forms of meningococcal disease such as meningococcemia. N. meningitidis is a major cause of morbidity and mortality in childhood in industrialized countries and is responsible for epidemics in Africa and in Asia. Approximately 2500 to 3500 cases of N meningitidis infection occur annually in the United States, with a case rate of about 1 in 100,000.
Thermotoga	Thermotoga are thermophile or hyperthermophile bacteria whose cell is wrapped in an outer "toga" membrane. They were named by microbiologist Karl Stetter. They metabolize carbohydrates.
Prochlorococcus	Prochlorococcus is a genus of very small (0.6 µm) marine cyanobacteria with an unusual pigmentation (chlorophyll b) belonging to photosynthetic picoplankton. It is probably the most abundant photosynthetic organism on Earth. Although there had been several earlier records of very small chlorophyll-b-containing cyanobacteria in the ocean, Prochlorococcus was actually discovered in 1986 by Sallie W. (Penny) Chisholm of the Massachusetts Institute of Technology, Robert J. Olson of the Woods Hole Oceanographic Institution, and other collaborators in the Sargasso Sea using flow cytometry.
Yersinia	Yersinia is a genus of bacteria in the family Enterobacteriaceae. Yersinia are Gram-negative rod shaped bacteria, a few micrometers long and fractions of a micrometer in diameter, and are facultative anaerobes. Some members of Yersinia are pathogenic in humans.
Neisseria gonorrhoeae	Neisseria gonorrhoeae or Gonococcus, is a species of Gram-negative kidney bean-shaped diplococci bacteria responsible for the sexually transmitted disease gonorrhoea. N.gonorrhoeae was first described by Albert Neisser in 1879. Neisseria are fastidious cocci, requiring nutrient supplementation to grow in laboratory cultures.
Pseudomonas	Pseudomonas is a genus of gamma proteobacteria, belonging to the larger family of pseudomonads. Recently, 16S rRNA sequence analysis has redefined the taxonomy of many bacterial species. As a result the genus Pseudomonas includes strains formerly classified in the genera Chryseomonas and Flavimonas.
Bacillus subtilis	Bacillus subtilis is a Gram-positive, catalase-positive bacterium commonly found in soil. A member of the genus Bacillus, B. subtilis is rod-shaped, and has the ability to form a tough, protective endospore, allowing the organism to tolerate extreme environmental conditions. Unlike several other well-known species, B. subtilis has historically been classified as an obligate aerobe, though recent research has demonstrated that this is not strictly correct.

Go to **Cram101.com** for Interactive Practice Exams for this book or virtually any of your books for $4.95/month.
And, **NEVER** highlight a book again!

Rhizobium	Rhizobium is a genus of Gram-negative soil bacteria that fix nitrogen. Rhizobium forms an endosymbiotic nitrogen fixing association with roots of legumes. The bacteria colonize plant cells within root nodules.
Rocky Mountain spotted fever	Rocky Mountain spotted fever is the most lethal and most frequently reported rickettsial illness in the United States. It has been diagnosed throughout the Americas. Some synonyms for Rocky Mountain spotted fever in other countries include "tick typhus," "Tobia fever" (Colombia), "São Paulo fever" or "febre maculosa" (Brazil), and "fiebre manchada" (Mexico.)
Nitrosomonadales	The Nitrosomonadales are a small order of Proteobacteria. They include Nitrosomonas, Nitrosospira, Gallionella (iron bacteria), and Spirillum.
Nitrosomonas	Nitrosomonas is a genus comprising of rod shaped chemoautotrophic bacteria. This rare bacteria oxidizes ammonia into nitrite as a metabolic process. Nitrosomonas are useful in treatment of industrial and sewage waste and in the process of bioremediation.
RecA	RecA is a 38 kilodalton Escherichia coli protein essential for the repair and maintenance of DNA. RecA has a structural and functional homolog in every species in which it has been seriously sought and serves as an archetype for this class of homologous DNA repair proteins. The homologous protein in Homo sapiens is called RAD51. RecA has multiple activities, all related to DNA repair.
Salmonella	Salmonella is a genus of rod-shaped, Gram-negative, non-spore forming, predominantly motile enterobacteria with diameters around 0.7 to 1.5 Âµm, lengths from 2 to 5 Âµm, and flagella which project in all directions (i.e. peritrichous.) They are chemoorganotrophs, obtaining their energy from oxidation and reduction reactions using organic sources and are facultative anaerobes; most species produce hydrogen sulfide, which can readily be detected by growing them on media containing ferrous sulfate, such as TSI. Most isolates exist in two phases; phase I is the motile phase and phase II the non-motile phase. Cultures that are non-motile upon primary culture may be swithched to the motile phase using a Craigie tube.
Staphylococcus	Staphylococcus is a genus of Gram-positive bacteria. Under the microscope they appear round , and form in grape-like clusters. The Staphylococcus genus include just thirty-three species.
Staphylococcus aureus	Staphylococcus aureus is the most common cause of staph infections. It is a spherical bacterium, frequently part of the skin flora found in the nose and on skin. About 20% of the population are long-term carriers of S. aureus.
Vibrio	Vibrio is a genus of Gram-negative bacteria possessing a curved rod shape. Typically found in saltwater, Vibrio are facultative anaerobes that test positive for oxidase and do not form spores. All members of the genus are motile and have polar flagella with sheaths.

Go to **Cram101.com** for Interactive Practice Exams for this book or virtually any of your books for $4.95/month.
And, **NEVER** highlight a book again!

Vibrio cholerae	Vibrio cholerae is a motile gram negative curved-rod shaped bacterium with a polar flagellum that causes cholera in humans. V. cholerae and other species of the genus Vibrio belong to the gamma subdivision of the Proteobacteria. There are two major strains of V. cholerae, classic and El Tor, and numerous other serogroups.
Salt	Salt played a major role during the Civil War. Salt not only preserved food in the days before refrigeration, but was also vital in the curing of leather. Union general William Tecumseh Sherman once said that "Salt is eminently contraband", as an army that has Salt can adequately feed its men.
Purple bacteria	Purple bacteria or purple photosynthetic bacteria are proteobacteria that are phototrophic, i.e. capable of producing energy through photosynthesis. They are pigmented with bacteriochlorophyll a or b, together with various carotenoids. These give them colours ranging between purple, red, brown, and orange.
Sulfolobus	In taxonomy, Sulfolobus is a genus of the Sulfolobaceae. Sulfolobus species grow in volcanic springs with optimal growth occurring at pH 2-3 and temperatures of 75-80 °C, making them acidophiles and thermophiles respectively. Sulfolobus cells are irregularly shaped and flagellar.
Purple sulfur bacteria	The Purple sulfur bacteria are a group of Proteobacteria capable of photosynthesis, collectively referred to as purple bacteria. They are anaerobic or microaerophilic, and are often found in hot springs or stagnant water. Unlike plants, algae, and cyanobacteria, they do not use water as their reducing agent, and so do not produce oxygen.
Paramyxovirus	Paramyxovirus es are viruses of the Paramyxoviridae family of the Mononegavirales order; they are negative-sense single-stranded RNA viruses responsible for a number of human and animal diseases. · Subfamily Paramyxovirinae · Genus Avulavirus (type species Newcastle disease virus) · Genus Henipavirus (type species Hendravirus; others include Nipahvirus) · Genus Morbillivirus (type species Measles virus; others include Rinderpest virus, Canine distemper virus, phocine distemper virus, Peste des Petits Ruminants virus (PPR)) · Genus Respirovirus (type species Sendai virus; others include Human parainfluenza viruses 1 and 3, as well some of the viruses of the common cold) · Genus Rubulavirus (type species Mumps virus; others include Human parainfluenza viruses 2 and 4, Simian parainfluenza virus 5, Menangle virus, Tioman virus) · Genus TPMV-like viruses (type species Tupaia Paramyxovirus · Subfamily Pneumovirinae · Genus Pneumovirus (type species Human respiratory syncytial virus, others include Bovine respiratory syncytial virus) · Genus Metapneumovirus (type species Avian pneumovirus, Human metapneumovirus) · Unassigned viruses

Go to **Cram101.com** for Interactive Practice Exams for this book or virtually any of your books for $4.95/month.
And, **NEVER** highlight a book again!

· Fer-de-Lance virus

· Nariva virus

· Tupaia Paramyxovirus

· Salem virus

· J virus

· Mossman virus

· Beilong virus

Virions are enveloped and can be spherical, filamentous or pleomorphic. Fusion proteins and attachment proteins appear as spikes on the virion surface. Matrix proteins inside the envelope stabilise virus structure.

Tir

Tir is an essential component in the binding of the pathogenic Escherichia coli strain EPEC (enteropathogenic E. coli) to the cells lining the small intestine. Tir is a receptor protein encoded by the espE gene which is located on the locus of enterocye effacement (LEE) pathogenicity island in EPEC strains. This receptor binds intimin upon translocation to enterocytes of the host cell.

Go to **Cram101.com** for Interactive Practice Exams for this book or virtually any of your books for $4.95/month.
And, **NEVER** highlight a book again!

Salt	Salt played a major role during the Civil War. Salt not only preserved food in the days before refrigeration, but was also vital in the curing of leather. Union general William Tecumseh Sherman once said that "Salt is eminently contraband", as an army that has Salt can adequately feed its men.
Neisseria	The Neisseria are a large family of commensal bacteria that colonize the mucosal surfaces of many animals. Of the eleven species that colonize humans, only two are pathogens. N. meningitidis and N. gonorrhoeae often cause asymptomatic infections, a commensal-like behavior.
Neisseria meningitidis	Neisseria meningitidis is a heterotrophic gram-negative diplococcal bacterium best known for its role in meningitis and other forms of meningococcal disease such as meningococcemia. N. meningitidis is a major cause of morbidity and mortality in childhood in industrialized countries and is responsible for epidemics in Africa and in Asia. Approximately 2500 to 3500 cases of N meningitidis infection occur annually in the United States, with a case rate of about 1 in 100,000.
Salmonella	Salmonella is a genus of rod-shaped, Gram-negative, non-spore forming, predominantly motile enterobacteria with diameters around 0.7 to 1.5 µm, lengths from 2 to 5 µm, and flagella which project in all directions (i.e. peritrichous.) They are chemoorganotrophs, obtaining their energy from oxidation and reduction reactions using organic sources and are facultative anaerobes; most species produce hydrogen sulfide, which can readily be detected by growing them on media containing ferrous sulfate, such as TSI. Most isolates exist in two phases; phase I is the motile phase and phase II the non-motile phase. Cultures that are non-motile upon primary culture may be swithched to the motile phase using a Craigie tube.
Psychrophiles	Psychrophiles or Cryophiles (adj. cryophilic) are extremophilic organisms that are capable of growth and reproduction in cold temperatures. They can be contrasted with thermophiles, which thrive at unusually hot temperatures.
Thermophile	A Thermophile is an organism -- a type of extremophile -- that thrives at relatively high temperatures, between 45 and 80 °C (113 and 176 °F.) Many Thermophile s are archaea. Thermophile s are found in various geothermally heated regions of the Earth such as hot springs like those in Yellowstone National Park and deep sea hydrothermal vents, as well as decaying plant matter such as peat bogs and compost.
Sulfolobus	In taxonomy, Sulfolobus is a genus of the Sulfolobaceae. Sulfolobus species grow in volcanic springs with optimal growth occurring at pH 2-3 and temperatures of 75-80 °C, making them acidophiles and thermophiles respectively. Sulfolobus cells are irregularly shaped and flagellar.
Pseudomonas	Pseudomonas is a genus of gamma proteobacteria, belonging to the larger family of pseudomonads. Recently, 16S rRNA sequence analysis has redefined the taxonomy of many bacterial species. As a result the genus Pseudomonas includes strains formerly classified in the genera Chryseomonas and Flavimonas.

Go to **Cram101.com** for Interactive Practice Exams for this book or virtually any of your books for $4.95/month.
And, **NEVER** highlight a book again!

Thermus aquaticus	Thermus aquaticus is a species of bacterium that can tolerate high temperatures, one of several thermophilic bacteria that belong to the Deinococcus-Thermus group. It is the source of the heat-resistant enzyme Taq DNA Polymerase, one of the most important enzymes in molecular biology because of its use in the polymerase chain reaction (PCR) DNA amplification technique.
	When studies of biological organisms in hot springs began in the 1960s, scientists thought that the life of thermophilic bacteria could not be sustained in temperatures above about 55° Celsius (131° Fahrenheit.)
Planctomycetes	Planctomycetes are a phylum of aquatic bacteria and are found in field samples of brackish, and marine and fresh water samples. They reproduce by budding. In structure, the organisms of this group are ovoid and have a holdfast, called the stalk, at the nonreproductive end that helps them to attach to each other during budding.
Shigella	Shigella is a genus of Gram-negative, non-spore forming rod-shaped bacteria closely related to Escherichia coli and Salmonella. The causative agent of human shigellosis, Shigella cause disease in primates, but not in other mammals. It is only naturally found in humans and apes.
Neisseria gonorrhoeae	Neisseria gonorrhoeae or Gonococcus, is a species of Gram-negative kidney bean-shaped diplococci bacteria responsible for the sexually transmitted disease gonorrhoea.
	N.gonorrhoeae was first described by Albert Neisser in 1879.
	Neisseria are fastidious cocci, requiring nutrient supplementation to grow in laboratory cultures.
Staphylococcus	Staphylococcus is a genus of Gram-positive bacteria. Under the microscope they appear round , and form in grape-like clusters.
	The Staphylococcus genus include just thirty-three species.
Staphylococcus aureus	Staphylococcus aureus is the most common cause of staph infections. It is a spherical bacterium, frequently part of the skin flora found in the nose and on skin. About 20% of the population are long-term carriers of S. aureus.
Streptobacillus	Streptobacillus is a genus of aerobic, gram-negative facultative anaerobe bacteria, which grow in culture as rods in chains.
	Species associated with infection - S. moniliformis
	Reported susceptibilities and therapies - penicillin, erythromycin
	Associated infections: the Haverhill fever form of rat bite fever. (Notes Spirillum minus is also an agent of rat bite fever, in the form known as sodoku.)
Streptococcal pharyngitis	Streptococcal pharyngitis or streptococcal sore throat is a form of group A streptococcal infection that affects the pharynx and possibly the larynx and tonsils.
	Streptococcal pharyngitis usually appears suddenly with a severe sore throat that may make talking or swallowing painful.
	Signs and symptoms may include

Go to **Cram101.com** for Interactive Practice Exams for this book or virtually any of your books for $4.95/month.
And, **NEVER** highlight a book again!

· Inflamed tonsils

· White spots on the tonsils

· Difficulty swallowing

· Tender cervical lymphadenopathy

· Fever

· Headache (often prior to other symptoms)

· Malaise, general discomfort, feeling ill or uneasy

· Halitosis

· Abdominal pain, nausea and vomiting

· Rash

· Hives

· Chills

· Loss of appetite

· Ear pain

· Peeling of skin on hands and feet

Additional symptoms such as sinusitis, vaginitis, or impetigo may be present if the strep bacteria infects both the throat and a secondary location. For additional information on non-pharynx symptoms, see Group A Streptococcal (GAS) Infection.

Tetanus

Tetanus is a medical condition characterized by a prolonged contraction of skeletal muscle fibers. The primary symptoms are caused by tetanospasmin, a neurotoxin produced by the Gram-positive, obligate anaerobic bacterium Clostridium tetani. Infection generally occurs through wound contamination and often involves a cut or deep puncture wound.

Go to **Cram101.com** for Interactive Practice Exams for this book or virtually any of your books for $4.95/month.
And, **NEVER** highlight a book again!

Salmonella	Salmonella is a genus of rod-shaped, Gram-negative, non-spore forming, predominantly motile enterobacteria with diameters around 0.7 to 1.5 µm, lengths from 2 to 5 µm, and flagella which project in all directions (i.e. peritrichous.) They are chemoorganotrophs, obtaining their energy from oxidation and reduction reactions using organic sources and are facultative anaerobes; most species produce hydrogen sulfide, which can readily be detected by growing them on media containing ferrous sulfate, such as TSI. Most isolates exist in two phases; phase I is the motile phase and phase II the non-motile phase. Cultures that are non-motile upon primary culture may be swithched to the motile phase using a Craigie tube.
Neisseria	The Neisseria are a large family of commensal bacteria that colonize the mucosal surfaces of many animals. Of the eleven species that colonize humans, only two are pathogens. N. meningitidis and N. gonorrhoeae often cause asymptomatic infections, a commensal-like behavior.
Neisseria gonorrhoeae	Neisseria gonorrhoeae or Gonococcus, is a species of Gram-negative kidney bean-shaped diplococci bacteria responsible for the sexually transmitted disease gonorrhoea. N.gonorrhoeae was first described by Albert Neisser in 1879. Neisseria are fastidious cocci, requiring nutrient supplementation to grow in laboratory cultures.
Pseudomonas	Pseudomonas is a genus of gamma proteobacteria, belonging to the larger family of pseudomonads. Recently, 16S rRNA sequence analysis has redefined the taxonomy of many bacterial species. As a result the genus Pseudomonas includes strains formerly classified in the genera Chryseomonas and Flavimonas.
Salt	Salt played a major role during the Civil War. Salt not only preserved food in the days before refrigeration, but was also vital in the curing of leather. Union general William Tecumseh Sherman once said that "Salt is eminently contraband", as an army that has Salt can adequately feed its men.
Tuberculosis	Tuberculosis is a common and often deadly infectious disease caused by mycobacteria, in humans mainly Mycobacterium Tuberculosis . Tuberculosis usually attacks the lungs (as pulmonary TB) but can also affect the central nervous system, the lymphatic system, the circulatory system, the genitourinary system, the gastrointestinal system, bones, joints, and even the skin. Other mycobacteria such as Mycobacterium bovis, Mycobacterium africanum, Mycobacterium canetti, and Mycobacterium microti also cause Tuberculosis, but these species are less common in humans.
Staphylococcus	Staphylococcus is a genus of Gram-positive bacteria. Under the microscope they appear round , and form in grape-like clusters. The Staphylococcus genus include just thirty-three species.
Streptobacillus	Streptobacillus is a genus of aerobic, gram-negative facultative anaerobe bacteria, which grow in culture as rods in chains. Species associated with infection - S. moniliformis Reported susceptibilities and therapies - penicillin, erythromycin Associated infections: the Haverhill fever form of rat bite fever. (Notes Spirillum minus is also an agent of rat bite fever, in the form known as sodoku.)

Go to **Cram101.com** for Interactive Practice Exams for this book or virtually any of your books for $4.95/month.
And, **NEVER** highlight a book again!

Shigella	Shigella is a genus of Gram-negative, non-spore forming rod-shaped bacteria closely related to Escherichia coli and Salmonella. The causative agent of human shigellosis, Shigella cause disease in primates, but not in other mammals. It is only naturally found in humans and apes.
Neisseria meningitidis	Neisseria meningitidis is a heterotrophic gram-negative diplococcal bacterium best known for its role in meningitis and other forms of meningococcal disease such as meningococcemia. N. meningitidis is a major cause of morbidity and mortality in childhood in industrialized countries and is responsible for epidemics in Africa and in Asia. Approximately 2500 to 3500 cases of N meningitidis infection occur annually in the United States, with a case rate of about 1 in 100,000.
Paenibacillus	Paenibacillus is a genus of bacteria, originally included within Bacillus. The name reflects this fact: Latin paene means almost, and so the Paenibacilli are literally almost Bacilli. The genus includes P. larvae, which causes American foulbrood in honeybees.
Yersinia	Yersinia is a genus of bacteria in the family Enterobacteriaceae. Yersinia are Gram-negative rod shaped bacteria, a few micrometers long and fractions of a micrometer in diameter, and are facultative anaerobes. Some members of Yersinia are pathogenic in humans.
Rhizobium	Rhizobium is a genus of Gram-negative soil bacteria that fix nitrogen. Rhizobium forms an endosymbiotic nitrogen fixing association with roots of legumes. The bacteria colonize plant cells within root nodules.

Go to **Cram101.com** for Interactive Practice Exams for this book or virtually any of your books for $4.95/month.
And, **NEVER** highlight a book again!

Shiga toxin	Shiga toxin s are a family of related toxins with two major groups, Stx1 and Stx2, whose genes are considered to be part of the genome of lambdoid prophages. The toxins are named for Kiyoshi Shiga, who first described the bacterial origin of dysentery caused by Shigella dysenteriae. The most common sources for Shiga toxin are the bacteria S. dysenteriae and the Shigatoxigenic group of Escherichia coli (Shiga toxin EC), which includes serotype O157:H7 and other enterohemorrhagic E. coli.
Staphylococcus	Staphylococcus is a genus of Gram-positive bacteria. Under the microscope they appear round , and form in grape-like clusters. The Staphylococcus genus include just thirty-three species.
Staphylococcus aureus	Staphylococcus aureus is the most common cause of staph infections. It is a spherical bacterium, frequently part of the skin flora found in the nose and on skin. About 20% of the population are long-term carriers of S. aureus.
Vancomycin-resistant	Vancomycin-resistant enterococcus (VRE) is the name given to a group of bacterial species of the genus Enterococcus that is resistant to the antibiotic vancomycin. Enterococci are enteric and can be found in the digestive and urinary tracts of some humans. VRE was discovered in 1985 and is particularly dangerous to immunocompromised individuals.
Vancomycin-resistant Staphylococcus aureus	Vancomycin-resistant Staphylococcus aureus is a strain of Staphylococcus aureus that has become resistant to the glycopeptide antibiotic vancomycin. With the increase of staphylococcal resistance to methicillin, vancomycin (or another antibiotic teicoplanin) is often a treatment of choice in infections with methicillin-resistant Staphylococcus aureus (MRSA.) Vancomycin resistance is still a rare occurrence.
Neisseria	The Neisseria are a large family of commensal bacteria that colonize the mucosal surfaces of many animals. Of the eleven species that colonize humans, only two are pathogens. N. meningitidis and N. gonorrhoeae often cause asymptomatic infections, a commensal-like behavior.
Neisseria meningitidis	Neisseria meningitidis is a heterotrophic gram-negative diplococcal bacterium best known for its role in meningitis and other forms of meningococcal disease such as meningococcemia. N. meningitidis is a major cause of morbidity and mortality in childhood in industrialized countries and is responsible for epidemics in Africa and in Asia. Approximately 2500 to 3500 cases of N meningitidis infection occur annually in the United States, with a case rate of about 1 in 100,000.
Salt	Salt played a major role during the Civil War. Salt not only preserved food in the days before refrigeration, but was also vital in the curing of leather. Union general William Tecumseh Sherman once said that "Salt is eminently contraband", as an army that has Salt can adequately feed its men.
Syphilis	Syphilis is a sexually transmitted disease caused by the spirochetal bacterium Treponema pallidum subspecies pallidum. The route of transmission of Syphilis is almost always through sexual contact, although there are examples of congenital Syphilis via transmission from mother to child in utero.

Go to **Cram101.com** for Interactive Practice Exams for this book or virtually any of your books for $4.95/month.
And, **NEVER** highlight a book again!

	The signs and symptoms of Syphilis are numerous; before the advent of serological testing, precise diagnosis was very difficult.
RecA	RecA is a 38 kilodalton Escherichia coli protein essential for the repair and maintenance of DNA. RecA has a structural and functional homolog in every species in which it has been seriously sought and serves as an archetype for this class of homologous DNA repair proteins. The homologous protein in Homo sapiens is called RAD51. RecA has multiple activities, all related to DNA repair.
Yersinia	Yersinia is a genus of bacteria in the family Enterobacteriaceae. Yersinia are Gram-negative rod shaped bacteria, a few micrometers long and fractions of a micrometer in diameter, and are facultative anaerobes. Some members of Yersinia are pathogenic in humans.
Thermotoga	Thermotoga are thermophile or hyperthermophile bacteria whose cell is wrapped in an outer "toga" membrane. They were named by microbiologist Karl Stetter. They metabolize carbohydrates.
Shigella	Shigella is a genus of Gram-negative, non-spore forming rod-shaped bacteria closely related to Escherichia coli and Salmonella. The causative agent of human shigellosis, Shigella cause disease in primates, but not in other mammals. It is only naturally found in humans and apes.
Salmonella	Salmonella is a genus of rod-shaped, Gram-negative, non-spore forming, predominantly motile enterobacteria with diameters around 0.7 to 1.5 µm, lengths from 2 to 5 µm, and flagella which project in all directions (i.e. peritrichous.) They are chemoorganotrophs, obtaining their energy from oxidation and reduction reactions using organic sources and are facultative anaerobes; most species produce hydrogen sulfide, which can readily be detected by growing them on media containing ferrous sulfate, such as TSI. Most isolates exist in two phases; phase I is the motile phase and phase II the non-motile phase. Cultures that are non-motile upon primary culture may be swithched to the motile phase using a Craigie tube.
Salmonella enterica	Salmonella enterica is a rod shaped, flagellated, aerobic, Gram-negative bacterium, and a member of the genus Salmonella. S. enterica has an extraordinarily large number of serovars or strains--up to 2000 have been described. · Salmonella enterica Serovar Typhi (historically elevated to species status as S. typhi) is the disease agent in typhoid fever. The genome sequences of Serovar Typhi has been established. · Salmonella enterica Serovar Typhimurium (also known as S. typhimurium) can lead to a form of human gastroenteritis sometimes referred to as salmonellosis. · The genome sequences of serovar Typhimurium LT2 have been established. Also an analysis of the proteome of Typhimurium LT2 under differing environmental conditions has been performed .

Go to **Cram101.com** for Interactive Practice Exams for this book or virtually any of your books for $4.95/month.
And, **NEVER** highlight a book again!

Nitrosomonadales	The Nitrosomonadales are a small order of Proteobacteria. They include Nitrosomonas, Nitrosospira, Gallionella (iron bacteria), and Spirillum.
Nitrosomonas	Nitrosomonas is a genus comprising of rod shaped chemoautotrophic bacteria. This rare bacteria oxidizes ammonia into nitrite as a metabolic process. Nitrosomonas are useful in treatment of industrial and sewage waste and in the process of bioremediation.
Rhizobium	Rhizobium is a genus of Gram-negative soil bacteria that fix nitrogen. Rhizobium forms an endosymbiotic nitrogen fixing association with roots of legumes. The bacteria colonize plant cells within root nodules.
Pseudomonas	Pseudomonas is a genus of gamma proteobacteria, belonging to the larger family of pseudomonads. Recently, 16S rRNA sequence analysis has redefined the taxonomy of many bacterial species. As a result the genus Pseudomonas includes strains formerly classified in the genera Chryseomonas and Flavimonas.
Veillonella	Veillonella are gram-negative anaerobic cocci. This bacterium is well known for its lactate fermenting abilities. They are a normal bacterium in the intestines and oral mucosa of mammals.
Transduction	Transduction is the process by which DNA is transferred from one bacterium to another by a virus. It also refers to the process whereby foreign DNA is introduced into another cell via a viral vector. This is a common tool used by molecular biologists to stably introduce a foreign gene into a host cell"s genome.
Tuberculosis	Tuberculosis is a common and often deadly infectious disease caused by mycobacteria, in humans mainly Mycobacterium Tuberculosis . Tuberculosis usually attacks the lungs (as pulmonary TB) but can also affect the central nervous system, the lymphatic system, the circulatory system, the genitourinary system, the gastrointestinal system, bones, joints, and even the skin. Other mycobacteria such as Mycobacterium bovis, Mycobacterium africanum, Mycobacterium canetti, and Mycobacterium microti also cause Tuberculosis, but these species are less common in humans.
Saccharomyces	Saccharomyces is a genus in the kingdom of fungi that includes many species of yeast. Saccharomyces is from Latin meaning sugar fungi. Many members of this genus are considered very important in food production.
Saccharomyces cerevisiae	Saccharomyces cerevisiae is a species of budding yeast. It is perhaps the most useful yeast owing to its use since ancient times in baking and brewing. It is believed that it was originally isolated from the skins of grapes
Bacillus anthracis	Bacillus anthracis is a Gram-positive spore-forming, rod-shaped bacterium, with a width of 1-1.2Âµm and a length of 3-5Âµm. It can be grown in an ordinary nutrient medium under aerobic or anaerobic conditions. It is the only bacterium with a protein capsule (D-glutamate), and the only pathogenic bacteria to carry its own adenylyl cyclase virulence factor (edema factor).

Go to **Cram101.com** for Interactive Practice Exams for this book or virtually any of your books for $4.95/month.
And, **NEVER** highlight a book again!

Klebsiella	Klebsiella is a genus of non-motile, Gram-negative, Oxidase-negative rod shaped bacteria with a prominent polysaccharide-based capsule. Frequent human pathogens, Klebsiella organisms can lead to a wide range of disease states, notably pneumonia, urinary tract infections, septicemia, ankylosing spondylitis, and soft tissue infections. Klebsiella species are ubiquitous in nature.
Sulfolobus	In taxonomy, Sulfolobus is a genus of the Sulfolobaceae. Sulfolobus species grow in volcanic springs with optimal growth occurring at pH 2-3 and temperatures of 75-80 °C, making them acidophiles and thermophiles respectively. Sulfolobus cells are irregularly shaped and flagellar.
Neisseria gonorrhoeae	Neisseria gonorrhoeae or Gonococcus, is a species of Gram-negative kidney bean-shaped diplococci bacteria responsible for the sexually transmitted disease gonorrhoea. N.gonorrhoeae was first described by Albert Neisser in 1879. Neisseria are fastidious cocci, requiring nutrient supplementation to grow in laboratory cultures.
Prevotella	Prevotella is a genus of bacteria. "Bacteroides melaninogenicus" has recently been reclassified and split into Prevotella melaninogenica and Prevotella intermedia. Several species have been implicated in oral disease.
Thermus aquaticus	Thermus aquaticus is a species of bacterium that can tolerate high temperatures, one of several thermophilic bacteria that belong to the Deinococcus-Thermus group. It is the source of the heat-resistant enzyme Taq DNA Polymerase, one of the most important enzymes in molecular biology because of its use in the polymerase chain reaction (PCR) DNA amplification technique. When studies of biological organisms in hot springs began in the 1960s, scientists thought that the life of thermophilic bacteria could not be sustained in temperatures above about 55° Celsius (131° Fahrenheit.)
Micrococcus	Micrococcus (mi" krÅ kÅ k" Æ s) is a genus of bacteria in the Micrococcaceae family. Micrococcus occurs in a wide range of environments, including water, dust, and soil. Micrococci have Gram-positive spherical cells ranging from about 0.5 to 3 micrometers in diameter and are typically appear in tetrads.
Bacillus subtilis	Bacillus subtilis is a Gram-positive, catalase-positive bacterium commonly found in soil. A member of the genus Bacillus, B. subtilis is rod-shaped, and has the ability to form a tough, protective endospore, allowing the organism to tolerate extreme environmental conditions. Unlike several other well-known species, B. subtilis has historically been classified as an obligate aerobe, though recent research has demonstrated that this is not strictly correct.

Go to **Cram101.com** for Interactive Practice Exams for this book or virtually any of your books for $4.95/month.
And, **NEVER** highlight a book again!

Planctomycetes	Planctomycetes are a phylum of aquatic bacteria and are found in field samples of brackish, and marine and fresh water samples. They reproduce by budding. In structure, the organisms of this group are ovoid and have a holdfast, called the stalk, at the nonreproductive end that helps them to attach to each other during budding.
Serratia	Serratia is a genus of Gram-negative, facultatively anaerobic, rod-shaped bacteria of the Enterobacteriaceae family. The most common species in the genus, S. marcescens, is normally the only pathogen and usually causes nosocomial infections. However, rare strains of S. plymuthica, S. liquefaciens, S. rubidaea, and S. odoriferae have caused diseases through infection.
Serratia marcescens	Serratia marcescens is a species of Gram-negative, rod-shaped bacteria in the family Enterobacteriaceae. A human pathogen, S. marcescens is involved in nosocomial infections, particularly catheter-associated bacteremia, urinary tract infections and wound infections, and is responsible for 1.4% of nosocomial bacteremia cases in the United States. It is commonly found in the respiratory and urinary tracts of hospitalized adults and in the gastrointestinal system of children.
Bacillus thuringiensis	Bacillus thuringiensis (or Bt) is a Gram-positive, soil-dwelling bacterium, commonly used as a pesticide. Additionally, B. thuringiensis also occurs naturally in the gut of caterpillars of various types of moths and butterflies, as well as on the dark surface of plants. B. thuringiensis was discovered 1901 in Japan by Ishiwata and 1911 in Germany by Ernst Berliner, who discovered a disease called Schlaffsucht in flour moth caterpillars.
Erythromycin	Erythromycin is a macrolide antibiotic that has an antimicrobial spectrum similar to or slightly wider than that of penicillin, and is often used for people who have an allergy to penicillins. For respiratory tract infections, it has better coverage of atypical organisms, including mycoplasma and Legionellosis. It was first marketed by Eli Lilly and Company, and it is today commonly known as EES (Erythromycin ethylsuccinate, an ester prodrug that is commonly administered).

Go to **Cram101.com** for Interactive Practice Exams for this book or virtually any of your books for $4.95/month.
And, **NEVER** highlight a book again!

Pseudomonas	Pseudomonas is a genus of gamma proteobacteria, belonging to the larger family of pseudomonads. Recently, 16S rRNA sequence analysis has redefined the taxonomy of many bacterial species. As a result the genus Pseudomonas includes strains formerly classified in the genera Chryseomonas and Flavimonas.
Syphilis	Syphilis is a sexually transmitted disease caused by the spirochetal bacterium Treponema pallidum subspecies pallidum. The route of transmission of Syphilis is almost always through sexual contact, although there are examples of congenital Syphilis via transmission from mother to child in utero. The signs and symptoms of Syphilis are numerous; before the advent of serological testing, precise diagnosis was very difficult.
Salmonella	Salmonella is a genus of rod-shaped, Gram-negative, non-spore forming, predominantly motile enterobacteria with diameters around 0.7 to 1.5 µm, lengths from 2 to 5 µm, and flagella which project in all directions (i.e. peritrichous.) They are chemoorganotrophs, obtaining their energy from oxidation and reduction reactions using organic sources and are facultative anaerobes; most species produce hydrogen sulfide, which can readily be detected by growing them on media containing ferrous sulfate, such as TSI. Most isolates exist in two phases; phase I is the motile phase and phase II the non-motile phase. Cultures that are non-motile upon primary culture may be swithched to the motile phase using a Craigie tube.
Thermophile	A Thermophile is an organism -- a type of extremophile -- that thrives at relatively high temperatures, between 45 and 80 °C (113 and 176 °F.) Many Thermophile s are archaea. Thermophile s are found in various geothermally heated regions of the Earth such as hot springs like those in Yellowstone National Park and deep sea hydrothermal vents, as well as decaying plant matter such as peat bogs and compost.
Neisseria	The Neisseria are a large family of commensal bacteria that colonize the mucosal surfaces of many animals. Of the eleven species that colonize humans, only two are pathogens. N. meningitidis and N. gonorrhoeae often cause asymptomatic infections, a commensal-like behavior.
Thermotoga	Thermotoga are thermophile or hyperthermophile bacteria whose cell is wrapped in an outer "toga" membrane. They were named by microbiologist Karl Stetter. They metabolize carbohydrates.
Thermus aquaticus	Thermus aquaticus is a species of bacterium that can tolerate high temperatures, one of several thermophilic bacteria that belong to the Deinococcus-Thermus group. It is the source of the heat-resistant enzyme Taq DNA Polymerase, one of the most important enzymes in molecular biology because of its use in the polymerase chain reaction (PCR) DNA amplification technique. When studies of biological organisms in hot springs began in the 1960s, scientists thought that the life of thermophilic bacteria could not be sustained in temperatures above about 55° Celsius (131° Fahrenheit.)
Stromatolite	Stromatolite s are layered accretionary structures formed in shallow water by the trapping, binding and cementation of sedimentary grains by biofilms of microorganisms, especially cyanobacteria (commonly known as blue-green algae.) They include some of the most ancient records of life on Earth.

Go to **Cram101.com** for Interactive Practice Exams for this book or virtually any of your books for $4.95/month.
And, **NEVER** highlight a book again!

	A variety of Stromatolite morphologies exist including conical, stratiform, branching, domal, and columnar types.
Bacillus sphaericus	Bacillus sphaericus is an obligate aerobe bacterium used as a larvicide for mosquito control. It forms spherical endospores. .
Norfloxacin	Norfloxacin is a synthetic chemotherapeutic agent occasionally used to treat common as well as complicated urinary tract infections. It is sold under various brand names with the most common being Noroxin. In form of ophthalmic solutions it is known as Chibroxin.
RecA	RecA is a 38 kilodalton Escherichia coli protein essential for the repair and maintenance of DNA. RecA has a structural and functional homolog in every species in which it has been seriously sought and serves as an archetype for this class of homologous DNA repair proteins. The homologous protein in Homo sapiens is called RAD51. RecA has multiple activities, all related to DNA repair.
Saccharomyces	Saccharomyces is a genus in the kingdom of fungi that includes many species of yeast. Saccharomyces is from Latin meaning sugar fungi. Many members of this genus are considered very important in food production.
Saccharomyces cerevisiae	Saccharomyces cerevisiae is a species of budding yeast. It is perhaps the most useful yeast owing to its use since ancient times in baking and brewing. It is believed that it was originally isolated from the skins of grapes
Neisseria gonorrhoeae	Neisseria gonorrhoeae or Gonococcus, is a species of Gram-negative kidney bean-shaped diplococci bacteria responsible for the sexually transmitted disease gonorrhoea. N.gonorrhoeae was first described by Albert Neisser in 1879. Neisseria are fastidious cocci, requiring nutrient supplementation to grow in laboratory cultures.
Proteus	Proteus is a genus of Gram-negative Proteobacteria. Three species--P. vulgaris, P. mirabilis, and P. penneri--are opportunistic human pathogens. Proteus includes pathogens responsible for many human urinary tract infections.
Proteus mirabilis	Proteus mirabilis is a Gram-negative, facultatively anaerobic bacterium. It shows swarming motility, and urease activity. P. mirabilis causes 90% of all "Proteus" infections in humans.
Serratia	Serratia is a genus of Gram-negative, facultatively anaerobic, rod-shaped bacteria of the Enterobacteriaceae family. The most common species in the genus, S. marcescens, is normally the only pathogen and usually causes nosocomial infections. However, rare strains of S. plymuthica, S. liquefaciens, S. rubidaea, and S. odoriferae have caused diseases through infection.

Go to **Cram101.com** for Interactive Practice Exams for this book or virtually any of your books for $4.95/month.
And, **NEVER** highlight a book again!

Serratia marcescens	Serratia marcescens is a species of Gram-negative, rod-shaped bacteria in the family Enterobacteriaceae. A human pathogen, S. marcescens is involved in nosocomial infections, particularly catheter-associated bacteremia, urinary tract infections and wound infections, and is responsible for 1.4% of nosocomial bacteremia cases in the United States. It is commonly found in the respiratory and urinary tracts of hospitalized adults and in the gastrointestinal system of children.
Staphylococcus	Staphylococcus is a genus of Gram-positive bacteria. Under the microscope they appear round , and form in grape-like clusters. The Staphylococcus genus include just thirty-three species.
Staphylococcus aureus	Staphylococcus aureus is the most common cause of staph infections. It is a spherical bacterium, frequently part of the skin flora found in the nose and on skin. About 20% of the population are long-term carriers of S. aureus.
Streptobacillus	Streptobacillus is a genus of aerobic, gram-negative facultative anaerobe bacteria, which grow in culture as rods in chains. Species associated with infection - S. moniliformis Reported susceptibilities and therapies - penicillin, erythromycin Associated infections: the Haverhill fever form of rat bite fever. (Notes Spirillum minus is also an agent of rat bite fever, in the form known as sodoku.)
Necrotizing fasciitis	Necrotizing fasciitis , commonly known as flesh-eating disease or flesh-eating bacteria, is a rare infection of the deeper layers of skin and subcutaneous tissues, easily spreading across the fascial plane within the subcutaneous tissue. Type I describes a polymicrobial infection, whereas Type II describes a monomicrobial infection. Many types of bacteria can cause Necrotizing fasciitis (eg.
Salmonella enterica	Salmonella enterica is a rod shaped, flagellated, aerobic, Gram-negative bacterium, and a member of the genus Salmonella. S. enterica has an extraordinarily large number of serovars or strains--up to 2000 have been described. · Salmonella enterica Serovar Typhi (historically elevated to species status as S. typhi) is the disease agent in typhoid fever. The genome sequences of Serovar Typhi has been established. · Salmonella enterica Serovar Typhimurium (also known as S. typhimurium) can lead to a form of human gastroenteritis sometimes referred to as salmonellosis. · The genome sequences of serovar Typhimurium LT2 have been established. Also an analysis of the proteome of Typhimurium LT2 under differing environmental conditions has been performed .

Go to **Cram101.com** for Interactive Practice Exams for this book or virtually any of your books for $4.95/month.
And, **NEVER** highlight a book again!

Rickettsia	Rickettsia is a genus of motile, Gram-negative, non-sporeforming, highly pleomorphic bacteria that can present as cocci (0.1 µm in diameter), rods (1-4 µm long) or thread-like (10 µm long.) Obligate intracellular parasites, the Rickettsia survival depends on entry, growth, and replication within the cytoplasm of eukaryotic host cells (typically endothelial cells.) Because of this, Rickettsia cannot live in artificial nutrient environments and are grown either in tissue or embryo cultures (typically, chicken embryos are used.)
Rickettsiales	The Rickettsiales are an order of small proteobacteria. Most of those described survive only as endosymbionts of other cells. Some are notable pathogens, including Rickettsia, which causes a variety of diseases in humans.

Go to **Cram101.com** for Interactive Practice Exams for this book or virtually any of your books for $4.95/month.
And, **NEVER** highlight a book again!

Prochlorococcus	Prochlorococcus is a genus of very small (0.6 µm) marine cyanobacteria with an unusual pigmentation (chlorophyll b) belonging to photosynthetic picoplankton. It is probably the most abundant photosynthetic organism on Earth. Although there had been several earlier records of very small chlorophyll-b-containing cyanobacteria in the ocean, Prochlorococcus was actually discovered in 1986 by Sallie W. (Penny) Chisholm of the Massachusetts Institute of Technology, Robert J. Olson of the Woods Hole Oceanographic Institution, and other collaborators in the Sargasso Sea using flow cytometry.
Syphilis	Syphilis is a sexually transmitted disease caused by the spirochetal bacterium Treponema pallidum subspecies pallidum. The route of transmission of Syphilis is almost always through sexual contact, although there are examples of congenital Syphilis via transmission from mother to child in utero. The signs and symptoms of Syphilis are numerous; before the advent of serological testing, precise diagnosis was very difficult.
Pseudomonas	Pseudomonas is a genus of gamma proteobacteria, belonging to the larger family of pseudomonads. Recently, 16S rRNA sequence analysis has redefined the taxonomy of many bacterial species. As a result the genus Pseudomonas includes strains formerly classified in the genera Chryseomonas and Flavimonas.
Proteobacteria	The Proteobacteria are a major group (phylum) of bacteria. They include a wide variety of pathogens, such as Escherichia, Salmonella, Vibrio, Helicobacter, and many other notable genera. Others are free-living, and include many of the bacteria responsible for nitrogen fixation.
Rickettsia	Rickettsia is a genus of motile, Gram-negative, non-sporeforming, highly pleomorphic bacteria that can present as cocci (0.1 µm in diameter), rods (1-4 µm long) or thread-like (10 µm long.) Obligate intracellular parasites, the Rickettsia survival depends on entry, growth, and replication within the cytoplasm of eukaryotic host cells (typically endothelial cells.) Because of this, Rickettsia cannot live in artificial nutrient environments and are grown either in tissue or embryo cultures (typically, chicken embryos are used.)
Rickettsia prowazekii	Rickettsia prowazekii is a species of gram negative, bacillus, obligate intracellular parasitic, aerobic bacteria that is the etiologic agent of epidemic typhus, transmitted in the feces of lice and fleas. In North America, the main reservoir for R. prowazekii is the flying squirrel. R. prowazekii is often surrounded by a protein microcapsular layer and slime layer; the natural life cycle of the bacterium generally involves a vertebrate and an invertebrate host, usually an arthropod, typically a louse.
Rickettsiales	The Rickettsiales are an order of small proteobacteria. Most of those described survive only as endosymbionts of other cells. Some are notable pathogens, including Rickettsia, which causes a variety of diseases in humans.

Go to **Cram101.com** for Interactive Practice Exams for this book or virtually any of your books for $4.95/month.
And, **NEVER** highlight a book again!

Rocky Mountain spotted fever	Rocky Mountain spotted fever is the most lethal and most frequently reported rickettsial illness in the United States. It has been diagnosed throughout the Americas. Some synonyms for Rocky Mountain spotted fever in other countries include "tick typhus," "Tobia fever" (Colombia), "São Paulo fever" or "febre maculosa" (Brazil), and "fiebre manchada" (Mexico.)
Typhus	Typhus is any of several similar diseases caused by Rickettsiae. The name comes from the Greek typhos meaning smoky or hazy,describing the state of mind of those affected with Typhus. The causative organism Rickettsia is an obligate parasite and cannot survive for long outside living cells.
Erwinia	Erwinia is a genus of Enterobacteriaceae bacteria containing mostly plant pathogenic species which was named for the first phytobacteriologist, Erwin Smith. It is a gram negative bacterium related to E.coli, Shigella, Salmonella and Yersinia. It is primarily a rod-shaped bacteria.
Rhizobium	Rhizobium is a genus of Gram-negative soil bacteria that fix nitrogen. Rhizobium forms an endosymbiotic nitrogen fixing association with roots of legumes. The bacteria colonize plant cells within root nodules.
Rhizobia	Rhizobia are soil bacteria that fix nitrogen (diazotrophy) after becoming established inside root nodules of legumes (Fabaceae.) Rhizobia require a plant host; they cannot independently fix nitrogen. Morphologically, they are generally gram negative, motile, non-sporulating rods.
Nitrosomonadales	The Nitrosomonadales are a small order of Proteobacteria. They include Nitrosomonas, Nitrosospira, Gallionella (iron bacteria), and Spirillum.
Nitrosomonas	Nitrosomonas is a genus comprising of rod shaped chemoautotrophic bacteria. This rare bacteria oxidizes ammonia into nitrite as a metabolic process. Nitrosomonas are useful in treatment of industrial and sewage waste and in the process of bioremediation.
Serratia	Serratia is a genus of Gram-negative, facultatively anaerobic, rod-shaped bacteria of the Enterobacteriaceae family. The most common species in the genus, S. marcescens, is normally the only pathogen and usually causes nosocomial infections. However, rare strains of S. plymuthica, S. liquefaciens, S. rubidaea, and S. odoriferae have caused diseases through infection.
Serratia marcescens	Serratia marcescens is a species of Gram-negative, rod-shaped bacteria in the family Enterobacteriaceae. A human pathogen, S. marcescens is involved in nosocomial infections, particularly catheter-associated bacteremia, urinary tract infections and wound infections, and is responsible for 1.4% of nosocomial bacteremia cases in the United States. It is commonly found in the respiratory and urinary tracts of hospitalized adults and in the gastrointestinal system of children.
Spirillum	Spirillum in microbiology refers to a bacterium with a cell body that twists like a spiral. It is the third distinct bacterial cell shape type besides coccus and bacillus cells. Spirillum is a genus of gram-negative bacteria.

Go to **Cram101.com** for Interactive Practice Exams for this book or virtually any of your books for $4.95/month.
And, **NEVER** highlight a book again!

Nitrifying bacteria	Nitrifying bacteria are chemoautotrophic bacteria that grow by consuming inorganic nitrogen compounds. Many species of Nitrifying bacteria have complex internal membrane systems that are the location for key enzymes in nitrification: ammonia monooxygenase which oxidizes ammonia to hydroxylamine, and nitrite oxidoreductase, which oxidizes nitrite to nitrate. Nitrifying bacteria are widespread in soil and water, and are found in highest numbers where considerable amounts of ammonia are present (areas with extensive protein decomposition, and sewage treatment plants.)
Neisseria	The Neisseria are a large family of commensal bacteria that colonize the mucosal surfaces of many animals. Of the eleven species that colonize humans, only two are pathogens. N. meningitidis and N. gonorrhoeae often cause asymptomatic infections, a commensal-like behavior.
Neisseria gonorrhoeae	Neisseria gonorrhoeae or Gonococcus, is a species of Gram-negative kidney bean-shaped diplococci bacteria responsible for the sexually transmitted disease gonorrhoea. N.gonorrhoeae was first described by Albert Neisser in 1879. Neisseria are fastidious cocci, requiring nutrient supplementation to grow in laboratory cultures.
Neisseria meningitidis	Neisseria meningitidis is a heterotrophic gram-negative diplococcal bacterium best known for its role in meningitis and other forms of meningococcal disease such as meningococcemia. N. meningitidis is a major cause of morbidity and mortality in childhood in industrialized countries and is responsible for epidemics in Africa and in Asia. Approximately 2500 to 3500 cases of N meningitidis infection occur annually in the United States, with a case rate of about 1 in 100,000.
Pertussis	Pertussis is a highly contagious disease caused by the bacterium Bordetella Pertussis It derived its name from the "whoop" sound made from the inspiration of air after a cough. A similar, milder disease is caused by B. para Pertussis .
Pseudomonadales	The Pseudomonadales are an order of Proteobacteria. A few members are opportunistic pathogens, such as species of Pseudomonas, Moraxella, and Acinetobacter, which may cause pneumonia. The bacterial genus Pseudomonas includes the opportunistic human pathogen P. aeruginosa, plant pathogenic bacteria, plant beneficial bacteria, ubiquitous soil bacteria with bioremediation capabilities and other species that cause spoilage of milk and dairy products.
Tularemia	Tularemia is a serious infectious disease caused by the bacterium Francisella tularensis. A gram-negative, non-motile coccobacillus, the bacterium has several subspecies with varying degrees of virulence. The most important of those is F. tularensis tularensis (Type A), which is found in lagomorphs in North America and is highly virulent for humans and domestic rabbits.

Go to **Cram101.com** for Interactive Practice Exams for this book or virtually any of your books for $4.95/month.
And, **NEVER** highlight a book again!

Q fever	Q fever is a disease caused by infection with Coxiella burnetii, a bacterium that affects both humans and animals. This organism is uncommon but may be found in cattle, sheep, goats and other domestic mammals, including cats and dogs. The infection results from inhalation of contaminated particles in the air, and from contact with the milk, urine, feces, vaginal mucus, or semen of infected animals.
Salmonella	Salmonella is a genus of rod-shaped, Gram-negative, non-spore forming, predominantly motile enterobacteria with diameters around 0.7 to 1.5 µm, lengths from 2 to 5 µm, and flagella which project in all directions (i.e. peritrichous.) They are chemoorganotrophs, obtaining their energy from oxidation and reduction reactions using organic sources and are facultative anaerobes; most species produce hydrogen sulfide, which can readily be detected by growing them on media containing ferrous sulfate, such as TSI. Most isolates exist in two phases; phase I is the motile phase and phase II the non-motile phase. Cultures that are non-motile upon primary culture may be swithched to the motile phase using a Craigie tube.
Vibrio	Vibrio is a genus of Gram-negative bacteria possessing a curved rod shape. Typically found in saltwater, Vibrio are facultative anaerobes that test positive for oxidase and do not form spores. All members of the genus are motile and have polar flagella with sheaths.
Vibrio parahaemolyticus	Vibrio parahaemolyticus is a curved, rod-shaped, Gram-negative bacterium found in brackish saltwater, which, when ingested, causes gastrointestinal illness in humans. V. parahaemolyticus is oxidase positive, facultatively aerobic, and does not form spores. Like other members of the genus Vibrio, this species is motile, with a single, polar flagellum.
Klebsiella	Klebsiella is a genus of non-motile, Gram-negative, Oxidase-negative rod shaped bacteria with a prominent polysaccharide-based capsule. Frequent human pathogens, Klebsiella organisms can lead to a wide range of disease states, notably pneumonia, urinary tract infections, septicemia, ankylosing spondylitis, and soft tissue infections. Klebsiella species are ubiquitous in nature.
Klebsiella pneumonia	Klebsiella pneumonia is a form of bacterial pneumonia associated with Klebsiella pneumoniae. It is typically due to aspiration by alcoholics, though it is more commonly implicated in hospital-acquired urinary tract and wound infections, particularly in immunocompromised individuals and diabetics. Patients with Klebsiella pneumonia tend to cough up a characteristic sputum that is said to resemble "red-currant jelly".
Proteus	Proteus is a genus of Gram-negative Proteobacteria. Three species--P. vulgaris, P. mirabilis, and P. penneri--are opportunistic human pathogens. Proteus includes pathogens responsible for many human urinary tract infections.

Go to **Cram101.com** for Interactive Practice Exams for this book or virtually any of your books for $4.95/month.
And, **NEVER** highlight a book again!

Proteus mirabilis	Proteus mirabilis is a Gram-negative, facultatively anaerobic bacterium. It shows swarming motility, and urease activity. P. mirabilis causes 90% of all "Proteus" infections in humans.
RecA	RecA is a 38 kilodalton Escherichia coli protein essential for the repair and maintenance of DNA. RecA has a structural and functional homolog in every species in which it has been seriously sought and serves as an archetype for this class of homologous DNA repair proteins. The homologous protein in Homo sapiens is called RAD51. RecA has multiple activities, all related to DNA repair.
Salmonella enterica	Salmonella enterica is a rod shaped, flagellated, aerobic, Gram-negative bacterium, and a member of the genus Salmonella. S. enterica has an extraordinarily large number of serovars or strains--up to 2000 have been described. · Salmonella enterica Serovar Typhi (historically elevated to species status as S. typhi) is the disease agent in typhoid fever. The genome sequences of Serovar Typhi has been established. · Salmonella enterica Serovar Typhimurium (also known as S. typhimurium) can lead to a form of human gastroenteritis sometimes referred to as salmonellosis. · The genome sequences of serovar Typhimurium LT2 have been established. Also an analysis of the proteome of Typhimurium LT2 under differing environmental conditions has been performed .
Shiga toxin	Shiga toxin s are a family of related toxins with two major groups, Stx1 and Stx2, whose genes are considered to be part of the genome of lambdoid prophages. The toxins are named for Kiyoshi Shiga, who first described the bacterial origin of dysentery caused by Shigella dysenteriae. The most common sources for Shiga toxin are the bacteria S. dysenteriae and the Shigatoxigenic group of Escherichia coli (Shiga toxin EC), which includes serotype O157:H7 and other enterohemorrhagic E. coli.
Shigella	Shigella is a genus of Gram-negative, non-spore forming rod-shaped bacteria closely related to Escherichia coli and Salmonella. The causative agent of human shigellosis, Shigella cause disease in primates, but not in other mammals. It is only naturally found in humans and apes.
Staphylococcus	Staphylococcus is a genus of Gram-positive bacteria. Under the microscope they appear round , and form in grape-like clusters. The Staphylococcus genus include just thirty-three species.
Staphylococcus aureus	Staphylococcus aureus is the most common cause of staph infections. It is a spherical bacterium, frequently part of the skin flora found in the nose and on skin. About 20% of the population are long-term carriers of S. aureus.

Go to **Cram101.com** for Interactive Practice Exams for this book or virtually any of your books for $4.95/month.
And, **NEVER** highlight a book again!

Salmonellosis	Salmonellosis is an infection with Salmonella bacteria. Most persons infected with salmonella develop diarrhea, fever, vomiting, and abdominal cramps; 12 to 72 hours after infection. In most cases, the illness lasts 3 to 7 days; most affected persons recover without treatment.
Shigellosis	Shigellosis is a foodborne illness caused by infection by bacteria of the genus Shigella. Shigellosis rarely occurs in animals other than humans and other primates like monkeys and chimpanzees. The causative organism is frequently found in water polluted with human feces, and is transmitted via the fecal-oral route.
Typhoid fever	Typhoid fever Salmonella typhi or commonly just typhoid, is an illness caused by the bacterium Salmonella enterica serovar typhi. Common worldwide, it is transmitted by the ingestion of food or water contaminated with feces from an infected person. The bacteria then perforate through the intestinal wall and are phagocytosed by macrophages.
Enterobacter aerogenes	Enterobacter aerogenes is a Gram-negative, oxidase negative, catalase positive, citrate positive, indole negative, rod-shaped bacterium. E. aerogenes is a nosocomial and pathogenic bacterium that causes opportunistic infections in skin and other tissues. Some strains can become very treatment resistant, a result of their colonization within hospital environments.
Pasteurella	Pasteurella is a genus of Gram-negative, facultatively anaerobic bacteria. Pasturella species are non-motile and pleomorphic. Most species are catalase- and oxidase-positive.
Pasteurella multocida	Pasteurella multocida is a Gram-negative, non-motile coccobacillus that is penicillin-sensitive and belongs to the Pasteurellaceae family . It can cause a zoonotic infection in humans, which typically is a result of bites or scratches from domestic pets. Many mammals and fowl harbor it as part of their normal respiratory microbiota, displaying asymptomatic colonization.
Yersinia	Yersinia is a genus of bacteria in the family Enterobacteriaceae. Yersinia are Gram-negative rod shaped bacteria, a few micrometers long and fractions of a micrometer in diameter, and are facultative anaerobes. Some members of Yersinia are pathogenic in humans.
Yersinia pestis	Yersinia pestis is a Gram-negative rod-shaped bacterium belonging to the family Enterobacteriaceae. It is a facultative anaerobe that can infect humans and other animals. Human Y. pestis infection takes three main forms: pneumonic, septicemic, and the notorious bubonic plagues.
Plague	Plague is a deadly infectious disease caused by the enterobacteria Yersinia pestis (Pasteurella pestis.) Plague is a zoonotic, primarily carried by rodents (most notably rats) and spread to humans via fleas. Plague is notorious throughout history, due to the unprecedented scale of death and devastation it brought.

Go to **Cram101.com** for Interactive Practice Exams for this book or virtually any of your books for $4.95/month.
And, **NEVER** highlight a book again!

Salt	Salt played a major role during the Civil War. Salt not only preserved food in the days before refrigeration, but was also vital in the curing of leather. Union general William Tecumseh Sherman once said that "Salt is eminently contraband", as an army that has Salt can adequately feed its men.
Purple sulfur bacteria	The Purple sulfur bacteria are a group of Proteobacteria capable of photosynthesis, collectively referred to as purple bacteria. They are anaerobic or microaerophilic, and are often found in hot springs or stagnant water. Unlike plants, algae, and cyanobacteria, they do not use water as their reducing agent, and so do not produce oxygen.
Tetanus	Tetanus is a medical condition characterized by a prolonged contraction of skeletal muscle fibers. The primary symptoms are caused by tetanospasmin, a neurotoxin produced by the Gram-positive, obligate anaerobic bacterium Clostridium tetani. Infection generally occurs through wound contamination and often involves a cut or deep puncture wound.
Bacillus anthracis	Bacillus anthracis is a Gram-positive spore-forming, rod-shaped bacterium, with a width of 1-1.2Âµm and a length of 3-5Âµm. It can be grown in an ordinary nutrient medium under aerobic or anaerobic conditions. It is the only bacterium with a protein capsule (D-glutamate), and the only pathogenic bacteria to carry its own adenylyl cyclase virulence factor (edema factor).
Bacillus cereus	Bacillus cereus is an endemic, soil-dwelling, Gram-positive, rod-shaped, beta hemolytic bacterium. Some strains are harmful to humans and cause foodborne illness, while other strains can be beneficial as probiotics for animals. It is the cause of "Fried Rice Syndrome".
Bacillus thuringiensis	Bacillus thuringiensis (or Bt) is a Gram-positive, soil-dwelling bacterium, commonly used as a pesticide. Additionally, B. thuringiensis also occurs naturally in the gut of caterpillars of various types of moths and butterflies, as well as on the dark surface of plants. B. thuringiensis was discovered 1901 in Japan by Ishiwata and 1911 in Germany by Ernst Berliner, who discovered a disease called Schlaffsucht in flour moth caterpillars.
Streptobacillus	Streptobacillus is a genus of aerobic, gram-negative facultative anaerobe bacteria, which grow in culture as rods in chains. Species associated with infection - S. moniliformis Reported susceptibilities and therapies - penicillin, erythromycin Associated infections: the Haverhill fever form of rat bite fever. (Notes Spirillum minus is also an agent of rat bite fever, in the form known as sodoku.)
Necrotizing fasciitis	Necrotizing fasciitis , commonly known as flesh-eating disease or flesh-eating bacteria, is a rare infection of the deeper layers of skin and subcutaneous tissues, easily spreading across the fascial plane within the subcutaneous tissue. Type I describes a polymicrobial infection, whereas Type II describes a monomicrobial infection. Many types of bacteria can cause Necrotizing fasciitis (eg.

Go to **Cram101.com** for Interactive Practice Exams for this book or virtually any of your books for $4.95/month.
And, **NEVER** highlight a book again!

Group B streptococcus	Infection with Group B Streptococcus can cause serious illness and sometimes death, especially in newborn infants, the elderly, and patients with compromised immune systems. Group B streptococci are also prominent veterinary pathogens, because they can cause bovine mastitis in dairy cows. The species name "agalactiae" meaning "no milk", alludes to this.
Rheumatic fever	Rheumatic fever is an inflammatory disease that may develop two to three weeks after a Group A streptococcal infection (such as strep throat or scarlet fever.) It is believed to be caused by antibody cross-reactivity and can involve the heart, joints, skin, and brain. Acute Rheumatic fever commonly appears in children ages 5 through 15, with only 20% of first time attacks occurring in adults.
Scarlet fever	Scarlet fever is a disease caused by an erythrogenic exotoxin released by Streptococcus pyogenes. The term Scarlatina may be used interchangeably with Scarlet fever, though it is commonly used to indicate the less acute form of Scarlet fever that is often seen since the beginning of the twentieth century. It is characterized by: · Sore throat · Fever · Bright red tongue with a "strawberry" appearance · Characteristic rash, which: · is fine, red, and rough-textured; it blanches upon pressure · appears 12-48 hours after the fever · generally starts on the chest, armpits, and behind the ears · spares the face · is worse in the skin folds. These are called Pastia lines (where the rash runs together in the arm pits and groins) appear and can persist after the rash is gone · may spread to cover the uvula. · The rash begins to fade three to four days after onset and desquamation (peeling) begins. "This phase begins with flakes peeling from the face.
Propionibacterium freudenreichii	Propionibacterium freudenreichii is a gram-positive, non-motile bacterium that plays an important role in the creation of emmental cheese, and to some extent, leerdammer. Its concentration in Swiss-type cheeses is higher than in any other cheese. Propionibacteria are commonly found in milk and dairy products, though they have also been extracted from soil.
Bacillus stearothermophilus	Bacillus stearothermophilus (or GeoBacillus stearothermophilus) is a rod-shaped, Gram-positive bacterium and a member of the division Firmicutes. The bacteria is a thermophile and is widely distributed in soil, hot springs, ocean sediment, and is a cause of spoilage in food products. It will grow within a temperature range of 30-75 degrees celsius.

Go to **Cram101.com** for Interactive Practice Exams for this book or virtually any of your books for $4.95/month.
And, **NEVER** highlight a book again!

Planctomycetes	Planctomycetes are a phylum of aquatic bacteria and are found in field samples of brackish, and marine and fresh water samples. They reproduce by budding. In structure, the organisms of this group are ovoid and have a holdfast, called the stalk, at the nonreproductive end that helps them to attach to each other during budding.
Prevotella	Prevotella is a genus of bacteria. "Bacteroides melaninogenicus" has recently been reclassified and split into Prevotella melaninogenica and Prevotella intermedia. Several species have been implicated in oral disease.
Psittacosis	In medicine, Psittacosis -- also known as parrot disease, parrot fever, and ornithosis -- is a zoonotic infectious disease caused by a bacterium called Chlamydophila psittaci and contracted not only from parrots, such as macaws, cockatiels and budgerigars, but also from pigeons, sparrows, ducks, hens, gulls and many other species of bird. The incidence of infection in canaries and finches is believed to be lower than in psittacine birds. The word "ornithosis" is only a synonym for "Psittacosis" in certain contexts : more generally the term is applied to any infection that is spread by birds.
Relapsing fever	Relapsing fever is an infection caused by certain bacteria in the genus Borrelia. It is a vector-borne disease that is transmitted through louse or soft-bodied tick bites. Borrelia recurrentis is the only agent of louse-borne disease.
Sulfolobus	In taxonomy, Sulfolobus is a genus of the Sulfolobaceae. Sulfolobus species grow in volcanic springs with optimal growth occurring at pH 2-3 and temperatures of 75-80 °C, making them acidophiles and thermophiles respectively. Sulfolobus cells are irregularly shaped and flagellar.
Thermophile	A Thermophile is an organism -- a type of extremophile -- that thrives at relatively high temperatures, between 45 and 80 °C (113 and 176 °F.) Many Thermophile s are archaea. Thermophile s are found in various geothermally heated regions of the Earth such as hot springs like those in Yellowstone National Park and deep sea hydrothermal vents, as well as decaying plant matter such as peat bogs and compost.
Thiomargarita namibiensis	Thiomargarita namibiensis is a gram-negative coccoid Proteobacterium, found in the ocean sediments of the continental shelf of Namibia. It is the largest bacterium ever discovered, generally 0.1 - 0.3 mm (100 - 300 µm) wide, but sometimes up to 0.75 mm (750 µm.) The genus name is formed from Greek θειον = sulfur , and Latin margarita = pearl.
Symbiotic bacteria	Symbiotic bacteria are bacteria living in symbiosis with another organism or each other. For example, Zoamastogopera, found in the stomach of termites, enable them to digest cellulose. Symbiotic bacteria are able to live in or on plant or animal tissue.

Go to **Cram101.com** for Interactive Practice Exams for this book or virtually any of your books for $4.95/month.
And, **NEVER** highlight a book again!

Neisseria	The Neisseria are a large family of commensal bacteria that colonize the mucosal surfaces of many animals. Of the eleven species that colonize humans, only two are pathogens. N. meningitidis and N. gonorrhoeae often cause asymptomatic infections, a commensal-like behavior.
Neisseria gonorrhoeae	Neisseria gonorrhoeae or Gonococcus, is a species of Gram-negative kidney bean-shaped diplococci bacteria responsible for the sexually transmitted disease gonorrhoea. N.gonorrhoeae was first described by Albert Neisser in 1879. Neisseria are fastidious cocci, requiring nutrient supplementation to grow in laboratory cultures.
Saccharomyces	Saccharomyces is a genus in the kingdom of fungi that includes many species of yeast. Saccharomyces is from Latin meaning sugar fungi. Many members of this genus are considered very important in food production.
Saccharomyces cerevisiae	Saccharomyces cerevisiae is a species of budding yeast. It is perhaps the most useful yeast owing to its use since ancient times in baking and brewing. It is believed that it was originally isolated from the skins of grapes
Staphylococcus	Staphylococcus is a genus of Gram-positive bacteria. Under the microscope they appear round , and form in grape-like clusters. The Staphylococcus genus include just thirty-three species.
Staphylococcus aureus	Staphylococcus aureus is the most common cause of staph infections. It is a spherical bacterium, frequently part of the skin flora found in the nose and on skin. About 20% of the population are long-term carriers of S. aureus.
Shigella	Shigella is a genus of Gram-negative, non-spore forming rod-shaped bacteria closely related to Escherichia coli and Salmonella. The causative agent of human shigellosis, Shigella cause disease in primates, but not in other mammals. It is only naturally found in humans and apes.
Pseudomonas	Pseudomonas is a genus of gamma proteobacteria, belonging to the larger family of pseudomonads. Recently, 16S rRNA sequence analysis has redefined the taxonomy of many bacterial species. As a result the genus Pseudomonas includes strains formerly classified in the genera Chryseomonas and Flavimonas.
Salmonella	Salmonella is a genus of rod-shaped, Gram-negative, non-spore forming, predominantly motile enterobacteria with diameters around 0.7 to 1.5 µm, lengths from 2 to 5 µm, and flagella which project in all directions (i.e. peritrichous.) They are chemoorganotrophs, obtaining their energy from oxidation and reduction reactions using organic sources and are facultative anaerobes; most species produce hydrogen sulfide, which can readily be detected by growing them on media containing ferrous sulfate, such as TSI. Most isolates exist in two phases; phase I is the motile phase and phase II the non-motile phase. Cultures that are non-motile upon primary culture may be swithched to the motile phase using a Craigie tube.
Streptobacillus	Streptobacillus is a genus of aerobic, gram-negative facultative anaerobe bacteria, which grow in culture as rods in chains.

Go to **Cram101.com** for Interactive Practice Exams for this book or virtually any of your books for $4.95/month.
And, **NEVER** highlight a book again!

	Species associated with infection - S. moniliformis Reported susceptibilities and therapies - penicillin, erythromycin Associated infections: the Haverhill fever form of rat bite fever. (Notes Spirillum minus is also an agent of rat bite fever, in the form known as sodoku.)
Vibrio	Vibrio is a genus of Gram-negative bacteria possessing a curved rod shape. Typically found in saltwater, Vibrio are facultative anaerobes that test positive for oxidase and do not form spores. All members of the genus are motile and have polar flagella with sheaths.
Rhizobium	Rhizobium is a genus of Gram-negative soil bacteria that fix nitrogen. Rhizobium forms an endosymbiotic nitrogen fixing association with roots of legumes. The bacteria colonize plant cells within root nodules.
Salt	Salt played a major role during the Civil War. Salt not only preserved food in the days before refrigeration, but was also vital in the curing of leather. Union general William Tecumseh Sherman once said that "Salt is eminently contraband", as an army that has Salt can adequately feed its men.
Thermus aquaticus	Thermus aquaticus is a species of bacterium that can tolerate high temperatures, one of several thermophilic bacteria that belong to the Deinococcus-Thermus group. It is the source of the heat-resistant enzyme Taq DNA Polymerase, one of the most important enzymes in molecular biology because of its use in the polymerase chain reaction (PCR) DNA amplification technique. When studies of biological organisms in hot springs began in the 1960s, scientists thought that the life of thermophilic bacteria could not be sustained in temperatures above about 55° Celsius (131° Fahrenheit.)
Planctomycetes	Planctomycetes are a phylum of aquatic bacteria and are found in field samples of brackish, and marine and fresh water samples. They reproduce by budding. In structure, the organisms of this group are ovoid and have a holdfast, called the stalk, at the nonreproductive end that helps them to attach to each other during budding.
Paramyxovirus	Paramyxovirus es are viruses of the Paramyxoviridae family of the Mononegavirales order; they are negative-sense single-stranded RNA viruses responsible for a number of human and animal diseases. · Subfamily Paramyxovirinae

Go to **Cram101.com** for Interactive Practice Exams for this book or virtually any of your books for $4.95/month.
And, **NEVER** highlight a book again!

· Genus Avulavirus (type species Newcastle disease virus)

· Genus Henipavirus (type species Hendravirus; others include Nipahvirus)

· Genus Morbillivirus (type species Measles virus; others include Rinderpest virus, Canine distemper virus, phocine distemper virus, Peste des Petits Ruminants virus (PPR))

· Genus Respirovirus (type species Sendai virus; others include Human parainfluenza viruses 1 and 3, as well some of the viruses of the common cold)

· Genus Rubulavirus (type species Mumps virus; others include Human parainfluenza viruses 2 and 4, Simian parainfluenza virus 5, Menangle virus, Tioman virus)

· Genus TPMV-like viruses (type species Tupaia Paramyxovirus

· Subfamily Pneumovirinae

· Genus Pneumovirus (type species Human respiratory syncytial virus, others include Bovine respiratory syncytial virus)

· Genus Metapneumovirus (type species Avian pneumovirus, Human metapneumovirus)

· Unassigned viruses

· Fer-de-Lance virus

· Nariva virus

· Tupaia Paramyxovirus

· Salem virus

· J virus

· Mossman virus

· Beilong virus

Virions are enveloped and can be spherical, filamentous or pleomorphic. Fusion proteins and attachment proteins appear as spikes on the virion surface. Matrix proteins inside the envelope stabilise virus structure.

Neisseria meningitidis	Neisseria meningitidis is a heterotrophic gram-negative diplococcal bacterium best known for its role in meningitis and other forms of meningococcal disease such as meningococcemia. N. meningitidis is a major cause of morbidity and mortality in childhood in industrialized countries and is responsible for epidemics in Africa and in Asia.
	Approximately 2500 to 3500 cases of N meningitidis infection occur annually in the United States, with a case rate of about 1 in 100,000.
Tularemia	Tularemia is a serious infectious disease caused by the bacterium Francisella tularensis. A gram-negative, non-motile coccobacillus, the bacterium has several subspecies with varying degrees of virulence. The most important of those is F. tularensis tularensis (Type A), which is found in lagomorphs in North America and is highly virulent for humans and domestic rabbits.
Prochlorococcus	Prochlorococcus is a genus of very small (0.6 µm) marine cyanobacteria with an unusual pigmentation (chlorophyll b) belonging to photosynthetic picoplankton. It is probably the most abundant photosynthetic organism on Earth.

Go to **Cram101.com** for Interactive Practice Exams for this book or virtually any of your books for $4.95/month.
And, **NEVER** highlight a book again!

Although there had been several earlier records of very small chlorophyll-b-containing cyanobacteria in the ocean, Prochlorococcus was actually discovered in 1986 by Sallie W. (Penny) Chisholm of the Massachusetts Institute of Technology, Robert J. Olson of the Woods Hole Oceanographic Institution, and other collaborators in the Sargasso Sea using flow cytometry.

Syphilis

Syphilis is a sexually transmitted disease caused by the spirochetal bacterium Treponema pallidum subspecies pallidum. The route of transmission of Syphilis is almost always through sexual contact, although there are examples of congenital Syphilis via transmission from mother to child in utero. The signs and symptoms of Syphilis are numerous; before the advent of serological testing, precise diagnosis was very difficult.

Spirillum

Spirillum in microbiology refers to a bacterium with a cell body that twists like a spiral. It is the third distinct bacterial cell shape type besides coccus and bacillus cells. Spirillum is a genus of gram-negative bacteria.

Go to **Cram101.com** for Interactive Practice Exams for this book or virtually any of your books for $4.95/month.
And, **NEVER** highlight a book again!

Serratia	Serratia is a genus of Gram-negative, facultatively anaerobic, rod-shaped bacteria of the Enterobacteriaceae family. The most common species in the genus, S. marcescens, is normally the only pathogen and usually causes nosocomial infections. However, rare strains of S. plymuthica, S. liquefaciens, S. rubidaea, and S. odoriferae have caused diseases through infection.
Serratia marcescens	Serratia marcescens is a species of Gram-negative, rod-shaped bacteria in the family Enterobacteriaceae. A human pathogen, S. marcescens is involved in nosocomial infections, particularly catheter-associated bacteremia, urinary tract infections and wound infections, and is responsible for 1.4% of nosocomial bacteremia cases in the United States. It is commonly found in the respiratory and urinary tracts of hospitalized adults and in the gastrointestinal system of children.
Phage therapy	Phage therapy is the therapeutic use of bacteriophages to treat pathogenic bacterial infections. Although extensively used and developed mainly in former Soviet Union countries for about 90 years, this method of therapy is still being tested elsewhere for treatment of a variety of bacterial and poly-microbial biofilm infections, and has not yet been approved in countries other than Georgia. Phage therapy has many potential applications in human medicine as well as dentistry, veterinary science, and agriculture.
Pseudomonas	Pseudomonas is a genus of gamma proteobacteria, belonging to the larger family of pseudomonads. Recently, 16S rRNA sequence analysis has redefined the taxonomy of many bacterial species. As a result the genus Pseudomonas includes strains formerly classified in the genera Chryseomonas and Flavimonas.
Viral plaque	A Viral plaque is a visible structure formed within a cell culture, such as bacterial cultures within some nutrient medium (e.g. agar.) The bacteriophage viruses replicate and spread, thus generating regions of cell destructions known as plaques. These plaques can sometimes be detected visually using colony counters, in much the same way as bacterial colonies are counted; however, they are not always visible to the naked eye, and sometimes can only be seen through a microscope, or using techniques such as staining or immunofluorescence.
Salt	Salt played a major role during the Civil War. Salt not only preserved food in the days before refrigeration, but was also vital in the curing of leather. Union general William Tecumseh Sherman once said that "Salt is eminently contraband", as an army that has Salt can adequately feed its men.
Shigella	Shigella is a genus of Gram-negative, non-spore forming rod-shaped bacteria closely related to Escherichia coli and Salmonella. The causative agent of human shigellosis, Shigella cause disease in primates, but not in other mammals. It is only naturally found in humans and apes.
Prevotella	Prevotella is a genus of bacteria. "Bacteroides melaninogenicus" has recently been reclassified and split into Prevotella melaninogenica and Prevotella intermedia. Several species have been implicated in oral disease.

Go to **Cram101.com** for Interactive Practice Exams for this book or virtually any of your books for $4.95/month.
And, **NEVER** highlight a book again!

Neisseria	The Neisseria are a large family of commensal bacteria that colonize the mucosal surfaces of many animals. Of the eleven species that colonize humans, only two are pathogens. N. meningitidis and N. gonorrhoeae often cause asymptomatic infections, a commensal-like behavior.
Neisseria gonorrhoeae	Neisseria gonorrhoeae or Gonococcus, is a species of Gram-negative kidney bean-shaped diplococci bacteria responsible for the sexually transmitted disease gonorrhoea. N.gonorrhoeae was first described by Albert Neisser in 1879. Neisseria are fastidious cocci, requiring nutrient supplementation to grow in laboratory cultures.
Shiga toxin	Shiga toxin s are a family of related toxins with two major groups, Stx1 and Stx2, whose genes are considered to be part of the genome of lambdoid prophages. The toxins are named for Kiyoshi Shiga, who first described the bacterial origin of dysentery caused by Shigella dysenteriae. The most common sources for Shiga toxin are the bacteria S. dysenteriae and the Shigatoxigenic group of Escherichia coli (Shiga toxin EC), which includes serotype O157:H7 and other enterohemorrhagic E. coli.
Streptobacillus	Streptobacillus is a genus of aerobic, gram-negative facultative anaerobe bacteria, which grow in culture as rods in chains. Species associated with infection - S. moniliformis Reported susceptibilities and therapies - penicillin, erythromycin Associated infections: the Haverhill fever form of rat bite fever. (Notes Spirillum minus is also an agent of rat bite fever, in the form known as sodoku.)
Transduction	Transduction is the process by which DNA is transferred from one bacterium to another by a virus. It also refers to the process whereby foreign DNA is introduced into another cell via a viral vector. This is a common tool used by molecular biologists to stably introduce a foreign gene into a host cell"s genome.
RecA	RecA is a 38 kilodalton Escherichia coli protein essential for the repair and maintenance of DNA. RecA has a structural and functional homolog in every species in which it has been seriously sought and serves as an archetype for this class of homologous DNA repair proteins. The homologous protein in Homo sapiens is called RAD51. RecA has multiple activities, all related to DNA repair.
Paramyxovirus	Paramyxovirus es are viruses of the Paramyxoviridae family of the Mononegavirales order; they are negative-sense single-stranded RNA viruses responsible for a number of human and animal diseases. · Subfamily Paramyxovirinae

Go to **Cram101.com** for Interactive Practice Exams for this book or virtually any of your books for $4.95/month.
And, **NEVER** highlight a book again!

· Genus Avulavirus (type species Newcastle disease virus)

· Genus Henipavirus (type species Hendravirus; others include Nipahvirus)

· Genus Morbillivirus (type species Measles virus; others include Rinderpest virus, Canine distemper virus, phocine distemper virus, Peste des Petits Ruminants virus (PPR))

· Genus Respirovirus (type species Sendai virus; others include Human parainfluenza viruses 1 and 3, as well some of the viruses of the common cold)

· Genus Rubulavirus (type species Mumps virus; others include Human parainfluenza viruses 2 and 4, Simian parainfluenza virus 5, Menangle virus, Tioman virus)

· Genus TPMV-like viruses (type species Tupaia Paramyxovirus

· Subfamily Pneumovirinae

· Genus Pneumovirus (type species Human respiratory syncytial virus, others include Bovine respiratory syncytial virus)

· Genus Metapneumovirus (type species Avian pneumovirus, Human metapneumovirus)

· Unassigned viruses

· Fer-de-Lance virus

· Nariva virus

· Tupaia Paramyxovirus

· Salem virus

· J virus

· Mossman virus

· Beilong virus

Virions are enveloped and can be spherical, filamentous or pleomorphic. Fusion proteins and attachment proteins appear as spikes on the virion surface. Matrix proteins inside the envelope stabilise virus structure.

Plague	Plague is a deadly infectious disease caused by the enterobacteria Yersinia pestis (Pasteurella pestis.) Plague is a zoonotic, primarily carried by rodents (most notably rats) and spread to humans via fleas. Plague is notorious throughout history, due to the unprecedented scale of death and devastation it brought.
Erwinia	Erwinia is a genus of Enterobacteriaceae bacteria containing mostly plant pathogenic species which was named for the first phytobacteriologist, Erwin Smith. It is a gram negative bacterium related to E.coli, Shigella, Salmonella and Yersinia. It is primarily a rod-shaped bacteria.

Go to **Cram101.com** for Interactive Practice Exams for this book or virtually any of your books for $4.95/month.
And, **NEVER** highlight a book again!

Yersinia	Yersinia is a genus of bacteria in the family Enterobacteriaceae. Yersinia are Gram-negative rod shaped bacteria, a few micrometers long and fractions of a micrometer in diameter, and are facultative anaerobes. Some members of Yersinia are pathogenic in humans.
Salmonella	Salmonella is a genus of rod-shaped, Gram-negative, non-spore forming, predominantly motile enterobacteria with diameters around 0.7 to 1.5 µm, lengths from 2 to 5 µm, and flagella which project in all directions (i.e. peritrichous.) They are chemoorganotrophs, obtaining their energy from oxidation and reduction reactions using organic sources and are facultative anaerobes; most species produce hydrogen sulfide, which can readily be detected by growing them on media containing ferrous sulfate, such as TSI. Most isolates exist in two phases; phase I is the motile phase and phase II the non-motile phase. Cultures that are non-motile upon primary culture may be swithched to the motile phase using a Craigie tube.
Salmonella enterica	Salmonella enterica is a rod shaped, flagellated, aerobic, Gram-negative bacterium, and a member of the genus Salmonella. S. enterica has an extraordinarily large number of serovars or strains--up to 2000 have been described. · Salmonella enterica Serovar Typhi (historically elevated to species status as S. typhi) is the disease agent in typhoid fever. The genome sequences of Serovar Typhi has been established. · Salmonella enterica Serovar Typhimurium (also known as S. typhimurium) can lead to a form of human gastroenteritis sometimes referred to as salmonellosis. · The genome sequences of serovar Typhimurium LT2 have been established. Also an analysis of the proteome of Typhimurium LT2 under differing environmental conditions has been performed .
Staphylococcus	Staphylococcus is a genus of Gram-positive bacteria. Under the microscope they appear round , and form in grape-like clusters. The Staphylococcus genus include just thirty-three species.
Staphylococcus aureus	Staphylococcus aureus is the most common cause of staph infections. It is a spherical bacterium, frequently part of the skin flora found in the nose and on skin. About 20% of the population are long-term carriers of S. aureus.
Prebiotics	Prebiotics are non-digestible food ingredients that stimulate the growth or activity of bacteria in the digestive system which are beneficial to the health of the body. They are considered a functional food. Typically, Prebiotics are carbohydrates (such as oligosaccharides), but the definition does not preclude non-carbohydrates.

Go to **Cram101.com** for Interactive Practice Exams for this book or virtually any of your books for $4.95/month.
And, **NEVER** highlight a book again!

Probiotics	Probiotics are dietary supplements of live microorganisms thought to be healthy for the host organism. According to the currently adopted definition by FAO/WHO, Probiotics are: "Live microorganisms which when administered in adequate amounts confer a health benefit on the host". Lactic acid bacteria (LAB) and bifidobacteria are the most common types of microbes used as Probiotics; but also certain yeasts and bacilli are available.
Bacillus anthracis	Bacillus anthracis is a Gram-positive spore-forming, rod-shaped bacterium, with a width of 1-1.2Âµm and a length of 3-5Âµm. It can be grown in an ordinary nutrient medium under aerobic or anaerobic conditions. It is the only bacterium with a protein capsule (D-glutamate), and the only pathogenic bacteria to carry its own adenylyl cyclase virulence factor (edema factor).
Bacillus stearothermophilus	Bacillus stearothermophilus (or GeoBacillus stearothermophilus) is a rod-shaped, Gram-positive bacterium and a member of the division Firmicutes. The bacteria is a thermophile and is widely distributed in soil, hot springs, ocean sediment, and is a cause of spoilage in food products. It will grow within a temperature range of 30-75 degrees celsius.
Neisseria	The Neisseria are a large family of commensal bacteria that colonize the mucosal surfaces of many animals. Of the eleven species that colonize humans, only two are pathogens. N. meningitidis and N. gonorrhoeae often cause asymptomatic infections, a commensal-like behavior.
Neisseria meningitidis	Neisseria meningitidis is a heterotrophic gram-negative diplococcal bacterium best known for its role in meningitis and other forms of meningococcal disease such as meningococcemia. N. meningitidis is a major cause of morbidity and mortality in childhood in industrialized countries and is responsible for epidemics in Africa and in Asia. Approximately 2500 to 3500 cases of N meningitidis infection occur annually in the United States, with a case rate of about 1 in 100,000.
Tuberculosis	Tuberculosis is a common and often deadly infectious disease caused by mycobacteria, in humans mainly Mycobacterium Tuberculosis . Tuberculosis usually attacks the lungs (as pulmonary TB) but can also affect the central nervous system, the lymphatic system, the circulatory system, the genitourinary system, the gastrointestinal system, bones, joints, and even the skin. Other mycobacteria such as Mycobacterium bovis, Mycobacterium africanum, Mycobacterium canetti, and Mycobacterium microti also cause Tuberculosis, but these species are less common in humans.
Erwinia	Erwinia is a genus of Enterobacteriaceae bacteria containing mostly plant pathogenic species which was named for the first phytobacteriologist, Erwin Smith. It is a gram negative bacterium related to E.coli, Shigella, Salmonella and Yersinia. It is primarily a rod-shaped bacteria.
RecA	RecA is a 38 kilodalton Escherichia coli protein essential for the repair and maintenance of DNA. RecA has a structural and functional homolog in every species in which it has been seriously sought and serves as an archetype for this class of homologous DNA repair proteins. The homologous protein in Homo sapiens is called RAD51. RecA has multiple activities, all related to DNA repair.

Go to **Cram101.com** for Interactive Practice Exams for this book or virtually any of your books for $4.95/month.
And, **NEVER** highlight a book again!

Shigella	Shigella is a genus of Gram-negative, non-spore forming rod-shaped bacteria closely related to Escherichia coli and Salmonella. The causative agent of human shigellosis, Shigella cause disease in primates, but not in other mammals. It is only naturally found in humans and apes.
Tetanus	Tetanus is a medical condition characterized by a prolonged contraction of skeletal muscle fibers. The primary symptoms are caused by tetanospasmin, a neurotoxin produced by the Gram-positive, obligate anaerobic bacterium Clostridium tetani. Infection generally occurs through wound contamination and often involves a cut or deep puncture wound.
Neisseria gonorrhoeae	Neisseria gonorrhoeae or Gonococcus, is a species of Gram-negative kidney bean-shaped diplococci bacteria responsible for the sexually transmitted disease gonorrhoea. N.gonorrhoeae was first described by Albert Neisser in 1879. Neisseria are fastidious cocci, requiring nutrient supplementation to grow in laboratory cultures.
Prevotella	Prevotella is a genus of bacteria. "Bacteroides melaninogenicus" has recently been reclassified and split into Prevotella melaninogenica and Prevotella intermedia. Several species have been implicated in oral disease.
Pseudomonas	Pseudomonas is a genus of gamma proteobacteria, belonging to the larger family of pseudomonads. Recently, 16S rRNA sequence analysis has redefined the taxonomy of many bacterial species. As a result the genus Pseudomonas includes strains formerly classified in the genera Chryseomonas and Flavimonas.
Prochlorococcus	Prochlorococcus is a genus of very small (0.6 Âµm) marine cyanobacteria with an unusual pigmentation (chlorophyll b) belonging to photosynthetic picoplankton. It is probably the most abundant photosynthetic organism on Earth. Although there had been several earlier records of very small chlorophyll-b-containing cyanobacteria in the ocean, Prochlorococcus was actually discovered in 1986 by Sallie W. (Penny) Chisholm of the Massachusetts Institute of Technology, Robert J. Olson of the Woods Hole Oceanographic Institution, and other collaborators in the Sargasso Sea using flow cytometry.
Vibrio	Vibrio is a genus of Gram-negative bacteria possessing a curved rod shape. Typically found in saltwater, Vibrio are facultative anaerobes that test positive for oxidase and do not form spores. All members of the genus are motile and have polar flagella with sheaths.
Vibrio cholerae	Vibrio cholerae is a motile gram negative curved-rod shaped bacterium with a polar flagellum that causes cholera in humans. V. cholerae and other species of the genus Vibrio belong to the gamma subdivision of the Proteobacteria. There are two major strains of V. cholerae, classic and El Tor, and numerous other serogroups.

Go to **Cram101.com** for Interactive Practice Exams for this book or virtually any of your books for $4.95/month.
And, **NEVER** highlight a book again!

Q fever	Q fever is a disease caused by infection with Coxiella burnetii, a bacterium that affects both humans and animals. This organism is uncommon but may be found in cattle, sheep, goats and other domestic mammals, including cats and dogs. The infection results from inhalation of contaminated particles in the air, and from contact with the milk, urine, feces, vaginal mucus, or semen of infected animals.
Shiga toxin	Shiga toxin s are a family of related toxins with two major groups, Stx1 and Stx2, whose genes are considered to be part of the genome of lambdoid prophages. The toxins are named for Kiyoshi Shiga, who first described the bacterial origin of dysentery caused by Shigella dysenteriae. The most common sources for Shiga toxin are the bacteria S. dysenteriae and the Shigatoxigenic group of Escherichia coli (Shiga toxin EC), which includes serotype O157:H7 and other enterohemorrhagic E. coli.
Pertussis	Pertussis is a highly contagious disease caused by the bacterium Bordetella Pertussis It derived its name from the "whoop" sound made from the inspiration of air after a cough. A similar, milder disease is caused by B. para Pertussis .
Shigellosis	Shigellosis is a foodborne illness caused by infection by bacteria of the genus Shigella. Shigellosis rarely occurs in animals other than humans and other primates like monkeys and chimpanzees. The causative organism is frequently found in water polluted with human feces, and is transmitted via the fecal-oral route.
Paramyxovirus	Paramyxovirus es are viruses of the Paramyxoviridae family of the Mononegavirales order; they are negative-sense single-stranded RNA viruses responsible for a number of human and animal diseases. · Subfamily Paramyxovirinae · Genus Avulavirus (type species Newcastle disease virus) · Genus Henipavirus (type species Hendravirus; others include Nipahvirus) · Genus Morbillivirus (type species Measles virus; others include Rinderpest virus, Canine distemper virus, phocine distemper virus, Peste des Petits Ruminants virus (PPR)) · Genus Respirovirus (type species Sendai virus; others include Human parainfluenza viruses 1 and 3, as well some of the viruses of the common cold) · Genus Rubulavirus (type species Mumps virus; others include Human parainfluenza viruses 2 and 4, Simian parainfluenza virus 5, Menangle virus, Tioman virus) · Genus TPMV-like viruses (type species Tupaia Paramyxovirus · Subfamily Pneumovirinae · Genus Pneumovirus (type species Human respiratory syncytial virus, others include Bovine respiratory syncytial virus) · Genus Metapneumovirus (type species Avian pneumovirus, Human metapneumovirus) · Unassigned viruses

Go to **Cram101.com** for Interactive Practice Exams for this book or virtually any of your books for $4.95/month.
And, **NEVER** highlight a book again!

· Fer-de-Lance virus

· Nariva virus

· Tupaia Paramyxovirus

· Salem virus

· J virus

· Mossman virus

· Beilong virus

Virions are enveloped and can be spherical, filamentous or pleomorphic. Fusion proteins and attachment proteins appear as spikes on the virion surface. Matrix proteins inside the envelope stabilise virus structure.

Klebsiella	Klebsiella is a genus of non-motile, Gram-negative, Oxidase-negative rod shaped bacteria with a prominent polysaccharide-based capsule. Frequent human pathogens, Klebsiella organisms can lead to a wide range of disease states, notably pneumonia, urinary tract infections, septicemia, ankylosing spondylitis, and soft tissue infections.
	Klebsiella species are ubiquitous in nature.
Klebsiella pneumonia	Klebsiella pneumonia is a form of bacterial pneumonia associated with Klebsiella pneumoniae.
	It is typically due to aspiration by alcoholics, though it is more commonly implicated in hospital-acquired urinary tract and wound infections, particularly in immunocompromised individuals and diabetics.
	Patients with Klebsiella pneumonia tend to cough up a characteristic sputum that is said to resemble "red-currant jelly".
Veillonella	Veillonella are gram-negative anaerobic cocci. This bacterium is well known for its lactate fermenting abilities. They are a normal bacterium in the intestines and oral mucosa of mammals.

Go to **Cram101.com** for Interactive Practice Exams for this book or virtually any of your books for $4.95/month.
And, **NEVER** highlight a book again!

Paramyxovirus	Paramyxovirus es are viruses of the Paramyxoviridae family of the Mononegavirales order; they are negative-sense single-stranded RNA viruses responsible for a number of human and animal diseases.

· Subfamily Paramyxovirinae

· Genus Avulavirus (type species Newcastle disease virus)
· Genus Henipavirus (type species Hendravirus; others include Nipahvirus)
· Genus Morbillivirus (type species Measles virus; others include Rinderpest virus, Canine distemper virus, phocine distemper virus, Peste des Petits Ruminants virus (PPR))
· Genus Respirovirus (type species Sendai virus; others include Human parainfluenza viruses 1 and 3, as well some of the viruses of the common cold)
· Genus Rubulavirus (type species Mumps virus; others include Human parainfluenza viruses 2 and 4, Simian parainfluenza virus 5, Menangle virus, Tioman virus)
· Genus TPMV-like viruses (type species Tupaia Paramyxovirus
· Subfamily Pneumovirinae

· Genus Pneumovirus (type species Human respiratory syncytial virus, others include Bovine respiratory syncytial virus)
· Genus Metapneumovirus (type species Avian pneumovirus, Human metapneumovirus)
· Unassigned viruses

· Fer-de-Lance virus
· Nariva virus
· Tupaia Paramyxovirus
· Salem virus
· J virus
· Mossman virus
· Beilong virus

Virions are enveloped and can be spherical, filamentous or pleomorphic. Fusion proteins and attachment proteins appear as spikes on the virion surface. Matrix proteins inside the envelope stabilise virus structure.

RecA	RecA is a 38 kilodalton Escherichia coli protein essential for the repair and maintenance of DNA. RecA has a structural and functional homolog in every species in which it has been seriously sought and serves as an archetype for this class of homologous DNA repair proteins. The homologous protein in Homo sapiens is called RAD51. RecA has multiple activities, all related to DNA repair.

Go to **Cram101.com** for Interactive Practice Exams for this book or virtually any of your books for $4.95/month.
And, **NEVER** highlight a book again!

Salmonella	Salmonella is a genus of rod-shaped, Gram-negative, non-spore forming, predominantly motile enterobacteria with diameters around 0.7 to 1.5 µm, lengths from 2 to 5 µm, and flagella which project in all directions (i.e. peritrichous.) They are chemoorganotrophs, obtaining their energy from oxidation and reduction reactions using organic sources and are facultative anaerobes; most species produce hydrogen sulfide, which can readily be detected by growing them on media containing ferrous sulfate, such as TSI. Most isolates exist in two phases; phase I is the motile phase and phase II the non-motile phase. Cultures that are non-motile upon primary culture may be swithched to the motile phase using a Craigie tube.
Shiga toxin	Shiga toxin s are a family of related toxins with two major groups, Stx1 and Stx2, whose genes are considered to be part of the genome of lambdoid prophages. The toxins are named for Kiyoshi Shiga, who first described the bacterial origin of dysentery caused by Shigella dysenteriae. The most common sources for Shiga toxin are the bacteria S. dysenteriae and the Shigatoxigenic group of Escherichia coli (Shiga toxin EC), which includes serotype O157:H7 and other enterohemorrhagic E. coli.
Vibrio	Vibrio is a genus of Gram-negative bacteria possessing a curved rod shape. Typically found in saltwater, Vibrio are facultative anaerobes that test positive for oxidase and do not form spores. All members of the genus are motile and have polar flagella with sheaths.
Vibrio cholerae	Vibrio cholerae is a motile gram negative curved-rod shaped bacterium with a polar flagellum that causes cholera in humans. V. cholerae and other species of the genus Vibrio belong to the gamma subdivision of the Proteobacteria. There are two major strains of V. cholerae, classic and El Tor, and numerous other serogroups.
Yersinia	Yersinia is a genus of bacteria in the family Enterobacteriaceae. Yersinia are Gram-negative rod shaped bacteria, a few micrometers long and fractions of a micrometer in diameter, and are facultative anaerobes. Some members of Yersinia are pathogenic in humans.
Yersinia pestis	Yersinia pestis is a Gram-negative rod-shaped bacterium belonging to the family Enterobacteriaceae. It is a facultative anaerobe that can infect humans and other animals. Human Y. pestis infection takes three main forms: pneumonic, septicemic, and the notorious bubonic plagues.
Plague	Plague is a deadly infectious disease caused by the enterobacteria Yersinia pestis (Pasteurella pestis.) Plague is a zoonotic, primarily carried by rodents (most notably rats) and spread to humans via fleas. Plague is notorious throughout history, due to the unprecedented scale of death and devastation it brought.
Shigellosis	Shigellosis is a foodborne illness caused by infection by bacteria of the genus Shigella. Shigellosis rarely occurs in animals other than humans and other primates like monkeys and chimpanzees. The causative organism is frequently found in water polluted with human feces, and is transmitted via the fecal-oral route.

Go to **Cram101.com** for Interactive Practice Exams for this book or virtually any of your books for $4.95/month.
And, **NEVER** highlight a book again!

Tuberculosis	Tuberculosis is a common and often deadly infectious disease caused by mycobacteria, in humans mainly Mycobacterium Tuberculosis . Tuberculosis usually attacks the lungs (as pulmonary TB) but can also affect the central nervous system, the lymphatic system, the circulatory system, the genitourinary system, the gastrointestinal system, bones, joints, and even the skin. Other mycobacteria such as Mycobacterium bovis, Mycobacterium africanum, Mycobacterium canetti, and Mycobacterium microti also cause Tuberculosis, but these species are less common in humans.
Typhoid fever	Typhoid fever Salmonella typhi or commonly just typhoid, is an illness caused by the bacterium Salmonella enterica serovar typhi. Common worldwide, it is transmitted by the ingestion of food or water contaminated with feces from an infected person. The bacteria then perforate through the intestinal wall and are phagocytosed by macrophages.
Neisseria	The Neisseria are a large family of commensal bacteria that colonize the mucosal surfaces of many animals. Of the eleven species that colonize humans, only two are pathogens. N. meningitidis and N. gonorrhoeae often cause asymptomatic infections, a commensal-like behavior.
Neisseria gonorrhoeae	Neisseria gonorrhoeae or Gonococcus, is a species of Gram-negative kidney bean-shaped diplococci bacteria responsible for the sexually transmitted disease gonorrhoea. N.gonorrhoeae was first described by Albert Neisser in 1879. Neisseria are fastidious cocci, requiring nutrient supplementation to grow in laboratory cultures.
Pseudomonas	Pseudomonas is a genus of gamma proteobacteria, belonging to the larger family of pseudomonads. Recently, 16S rRNA sequence analysis has redefined the taxonomy of many bacterial species. As a result the genus Pseudomonas includes strains formerly classified in the genera Chryseomonas and Flavimonas.
Shigella	Shigella is a genus of Gram-negative, non-spore forming rod-shaped bacteria closely related to Escherichia coli and Salmonella. The causative agent of human shigellosis, Shigella cause disease in primates, but not in other mammals. It is only naturally found in humans and apes.
Syphilis	Syphilis is a sexually transmitted disease caused by the spirochetal bacterium Treponema pallidum subspecies pallidum. The route of transmission of Syphilis is almost always through sexual contact, although there are examples of congenital Syphilis via transmission from mother to child in utero. The signs and symptoms of Syphilis are numerous; before the advent of serological testing, precise diagnosis was very difficult.
Bacillus anthracis	Bacillus anthracis is a Gram-positive spore-forming, rod-shaped bacterium, with a width of 1-1.2Âµm and a length of 3-5Âµm. It can be grown in an ordinary nutrient medium under aerobic or anaerobic conditions. It is the only bacterium with a protein capsule (D-glutamate), and the only pathogenic bacteria to carry its own adenylyl cyclase virulence factor (edema factor).
Staphylococcus	Staphylococcus is a genus of Gram-positive bacteria. Under the microscope they appear round , and form in grape-like clusters.

Go to **Cram101.com** for Interactive Practice Exams for this book or virtually any of your books for $4.95/month.
And, **NEVER** highlight a book again!

The Staphylococcus genus include just thirty-three species.

Staphylococcus aureus	Staphylococcus aureus is the most common cause of staph infections. It is a spherical bacterium, frequently part of the skin flora found in the nose and on skin. About 20% of the population are long-term carriers of S. aureus.
Thermotoga	Thermotoga are thermophile or hyperthermophile bacteria whose cell is wrapped in an outer "toga" membrane. They were named by microbiologist Karl Stetter. They metabolize carbohydrates.
Staphylokinase	Staphylokinase (SAK) is a amino acid enzyme from Staphylococcus aureus. It is positively regulated by the "agr" gene regulator. It activates plasminogen to form plasmin, which digest fibrin clots.
Neisseria meningitidis	Neisseria meningitidis is a heterotrophic gram-negative diplococcal bacterium best known for its role in meningitis and other forms of meningococcal disease such as meningococcemia. N. meningitidis is a major cause of morbidity and mortality in childhood in industrialized countries and is responsible for epidemics in Africa and in Asia. Approximately 2500 to 3500 cases of N meningitidis infection occur annually in the United States, with a case rate of about 1 in 100,000.
Tetanus	Tetanus is a medical condition characterized by a prolonged contraction of skeletal muscle fibers. The primary symptoms are caused by tetanospasmin, a neurotoxin produced by the Gram-positive, obligate anaerobic bacterium Clostridium tetani. Infection generally occurs through wound contamination and often involves a cut or deep puncture wound.
Scarlet fever	Scarlet fever is a disease caused by an erythrogenic exotoxin released by Streptococcus pyogenes. The term Scarlatina may be used interchangeably with Scarlet fever, though it is commonly used to indicate the less acute form of Scarlet fever that is often seen since the beginning of the twentieth century. It is characterized by: · Sore throat · Fever · Bright red tongue with a "strawberry" appearance · Characteristic rash, which: · is fine, red, and rough-textured; it blanches upon pressure · appears 12-48 hours after the fever · generally starts on the chest, armpits, and behind the ears · spares the face · is worse in the skin folds. These are called Pastia lines (where the rash runs together in the arm pits and groins) appear and can persist after the rash is gone · may spread to cover the uvula.

Go to **Cram101.com** for Interactive Practice Exams for this book or virtually any of your books for $4.95/month.
And, **NEVER** highlight a book again!

· The rash begins to fade three to four days after onset and desquamation (peeling) begins. "This phase begins with flakes peeling from the face.

Proteus

Proteus is a genus of Gram-negative Proteobacteria.

Three species--P. vulgaris, P. mirabilis, and P. penneri--are opportunistic human pathogens. Proteus includes pathogens responsible for many human urinary tract infections.

Go to **Cram101.com** for Interactive Practice Exams for this book or virtually any of your books for $4.95/month.
And, **NEVER** highlight a book again!

Pseudomonas	Pseudomonas is a genus of gamma proteobacteria, belonging to the larger family of pseudomonads. Recently, 16S rRNA sequence analysis has redefined the taxonomy of many bacterial species. As a result the genus Pseudomonas includes strains formerly classified in the genera Chryseomonas and Flavimonas.
Staphylococcus	Staphylococcus is a genus of Gram-positive bacteria. Under the microscope they appear round , and form in grape-like clusters. The Staphylococcus genus include just thirty-three species.
Yersinia	Yersinia is a genus of bacteria in the family Enterobacteriaceae. Yersinia are Gram-negative rod shaped bacteria, a few micrometers long and fractions of a micrometer in diameter, and are facultative anaerobes. Some members of Yersinia are pathogenic in humans.
Periplasmic space	The Periplasmic space or periplasm is a space between the inner cytoplasmic membrane and external outer membrane of Gram-negative bacteria or the equivalent space between the cell membrane and cell wall in Gram-positive bacteria. It may constitute up to 40% of the total cell volume in Gram-negative species, and is drastically smaller in Gram-positive. The space contains a loose network of murein (peptidoglycan) chains, as well as a gel containing hydrolytic and degradative enzymes.
RecA	RecA is a 38 kilodalton Escherichia coli protein essential for the repair and maintenance of DNA. RecA has a structural and functional homolog in every species in which it has been seriously sought and serves as an archetype for this class of homologous DNA repair proteins. The homologous protein in Homo sapiens is called RAD51. RecA has multiple activities, all related to DNA repair.
Staphylococcus aureus	Staphylococcus aureus is the most common cause of staph infections. It is a spherical bacterium, frequently part of the skin flora found in the nose and on skin. About 20% of the population are long-term carriers of S. aureus.
Vancomycin-resistant	Vancomycin-resistant enterococcus (VRE) is the name given to a group of bacterial species of the genus Enterococcus that is resistant to the antibiotic vancomycin. Enterococci are enteric and can be found in the digestive and urinary tracts of some humans. VRE was discovered in 1985 and is particularly dangerous to immunocompromised individuals.
Micrococcus	Micrococcus (mi" krÅ kÅ k" Æ s) is a genus of bacteria in the Micrococcaceae family. Micrococcus occurs in a wide range of environments, including water, dust, and soil. Micrococci have Gram-positive spherical cells ranging from about 0.5 to 3 micrometers in diameter and are typically appear in tetrads.
Spirillum	Spirillum in microbiology refers to a bacterium with a cell body that twists like a spiral. It is the third distinct bacterial cell shape type besides coccus and bacillus cells. Spirillum is a genus of gram-negative bacteria.

Go to **Cram101.com** for Interactive Practice Exams for this book or virtually any of your books for $4.95/month.
And, **NEVER** highlight a book again!

Neisseria	The Neisseria are a large family of commensal bacteria that colonize the mucosal surfaces of many animals. Of the eleven species that colonize humans, only two are pathogens. N. meningitidis and N. gonorrhoeae often cause asymptomatic infections, a commensal-like behavior.
Neisseria gonorrhoeae	Neisseria gonorrhoeae or Gonococcus, is a species of Gram-negative kidney bean-shaped diplococci bacteria responsible for the sexually transmitted disease gonorrhoea. N.gonorrhoeae was first described by Albert Neisser in 1879. Neisseria are fastidious cocci, requiring nutrient supplementation to grow in laboratory cultures.
Q fever	Q fever is a disease caused by infection with Coxiella burnetii, a bacterium that affects both humans and animals. This organism is uncommon but may be found in cattle, sheep, goats and other domestic mammals, including cats and dogs. The infection results from inhalation of contaminated particles in the air, and from contact with the milk, urine, feces, vaginal mucus, or semen of infected animals.
Rocky Mountain spotted fever	Rocky Mountain spotted fever is the most lethal and most frequently reported rickettsial illness in the United States. It has been diagnosed throughout the Americas. Some synonyms for Rocky Mountain spotted fever in other countries include "tick typhus," "Tobia fever" (Colombia), "São Paulo fever" or "febre maculosa" (Brazil), and "fiebre manchada" (Mexico.)
Shiga toxin	Shiga toxin s are a family of related toxins with two major groups, Stx1 and Stx2, whose genes are considered to be part of the genome of lambdoid prophages. The toxins are named for Kiyoshi Shiga, who first described the bacterial origin of dysentery caused by Shigella dysenteriae. The most common sources for Shiga toxin are the bacteria S. dysenteriae and the Shigatoxigenic group of Escherichia coli (Shiga toxin EC), which includes serotype O157:H7 and other enterohemorrhagic E. coli.
Tuberculosis	Tuberculosis is a common and often deadly infectious disease caused by mycobacteria, in humans mainly Mycobacterium Tuberculosis . Tuberculosis usually attacks the lungs (as pulmonary TB) but can also affect the central nervous system, the lymphatic system, the circulatory system, the genitourinary system, the gastrointestinal system, bones, joints, and even the skin. Other mycobacteria such as Mycobacterium bovis, Mycobacterium africanum, Mycobacterium canetti, and Mycobacterium microti also cause Tuberculosis, but these species are less common in humans.
Typhus	Typhus is any of several similar diseases caused by Rickettsiae. The name comes from the Greek typhos meaning smoky or hazy,describing the state of mind of those affected with Typhus. The causative organism Rickettsia is an obligate parasite and cannot survive for long outside living cells.
Paenibacillus	Paenibacillus is a genus of bacteria, originally included within Bacillus. The name reflects this fact: Latin paene means almost, and so the Paenibacilli are literally almost Bacilli. The genus includes P. larvae, which causes American foulbrood in honeybees.

Go to **Cram101.com** for Interactive Practice Exams for this book or virtually any of your books for $4.95/month.
And, **NEVER** highlight a book again!

Shigella	Shigella is a genus of Gram-negative, non-spore forming rod-shaped bacteria closely related to Escherichia coli and Salmonella. The causative agent of human shigellosis, Shigella cause disease in primates, but not in other mammals. It is only naturally found in humans and apes.
Pertussis	Pertussis is a highly contagious disease caused by the bacterium Bordetella Pertussis It derived its name from the "whoop" sound made from the inspiration of air after a cough. A similar, milder disease is caused by B. para Pertussis .
Neisseria meningitidis	Neisseria meningitidis is a heterotrophic gram-negative diplococcal bacterium best known for its role in meningitis and other forms of meningococcal disease such as meningococcemia. N. meningitidis is a major cause of morbidity and mortality in childhood in industrialized countries and is responsible for epidemics in Africa and in Asia. Approximately 2500 to 3500 cases of N meningitidis infection occur annually in the United States, with a case rate of about 1 in 100,000.
Rickettsiales	The Rickettsiales are an order of small proteobacteria. Most of those described survive only as endosymbionts of other cells. Some are notable pathogens, including Rickettsia, which causes a variety of diseases in humans.

Go to **Cram101.com** for Interactive Practice Exams for this book or virtually any of your books for $4.95/month.
And, **NEVER** highlight a book again!

Bacillus stearothermophilus	Bacillus stearothermophilus (or GeoBacillus stearothermophilus) is a rod-shaped, Gram-positive bacterium and a member of the division Firmicutes. The bacteria is a thermophile and is widely distributed in soil, hot springs, ocean sediment, and is a cause of spoilage in food products. It will grow within a temperature range of 30-75 degrees celsius.
Pseudomonas	Pseudomonas is a genus of gamma proteobacteria, belonging to the larger family of pseudomonads. Recently, 16S rRNA sequence analysis has redefined the taxonomy of many bacterial species. As a result the genus Pseudomonas includes strains formerly classified in the genera Chryseomonas and Flavimonas.
Neisseria	The Neisseria are a large family of commensal bacteria that colonize the mucosal surfaces of many animals. Of the eleven species that colonize humans, only two are pathogens. N. meningitidis and N. gonorrhoeae often cause asymptomatic infections, a commensal-like behavior.
Neisseria gonorrhoeae	Neisseria gonorrhoeae or Gonococcus, is a species of Gram-negative kidney bean-shaped diplococci bacteria responsible for the sexually transmitted disease gonorrhoea. N.gonorrhoeae was first described by Albert Neisser in 1879. Neisseria are fastidious cocci, requiring nutrient supplementation to grow in laboratory cultures.
Serratia	Serratia is a genus of Gram-negative, facultatively anaerobic, rod-shaped bacteria of the Enterobacteriaceae family. The most common species in the genus, S. marcescens, is normally the only pathogen and usually causes nosocomial infections. However, rare strains of S. plymuthica, S. liquefaciens, S. rubidaea, and S. odoriferae have caused diseases through infection.
Serratia marcescens	Serratia marcescens is a species of Gram-negative, rod-shaped bacteria in the family Enterobacteriaceae. A human pathogen, S. marcescens is involved in nosocomial infections, particularly catheter-associated bacteremia, urinary tract infections and wound infections, and is responsible for 1.4% of nosocomial bacteremia cases in the United States. It is commonly found in the respiratory and urinary tracts of hospitalized adults and in the gastrointestinal system of children.
Prochlorococcus	Prochlorococcus is a genus of very small (0.6 µm) marine cyanobacteria with an unusual pigmentation (chlorophyll b) belonging to photosynthetic picoplankton. It is probably the most abundant photosynthetic organism on Earth. Although there had been several earlier records of very small chlorophyll-b-containing cyanobacteria in the ocean, Prochlorococcus was actually discovered in 1986 by Sallie W. (Penny) Chisholm of the Massachusetts Institute of Technology, Robert J. Olson of the Woods Hole Oceanographic Institution, and other collaborators in the Sargasso Sea using flow cytometry.

Go to **Cram101.com** for Interactive Practice Exams for this book or virtually any of your books for $4.95/month.
And, **NEVER** highlight a book again!

Salmonella	Salmonella is a genus of rod-shaped, Gram-negative, non-spore forming, predominantly motile enterobacteria with diameters around 0.7 to 1.5 µm, lengths from 2 to 5 µm, and flagella which project in all directions (i.e. peritrichous.) They are chemoorganotrophs, obtaining their energy from oxidation and reduction reactions using organic sources and are facultative anaerobes; most species produce hydrogen sulfide, which can readily be detected by growing them on media containing ferrous sulfate, such as TSI. Most isolates exist in two phases; phase I is the motile phase and phase II the non-motile phase. Cultures that are non-motile upon primary culture may be swithched to the motile phase using a Craigie tube.
Prevotella	Prevotella is a genus of bacteria. "Bacteroides melaninogenicus" has recently been reclassified and split into Prevotella melaninogenica and Prevotella intermedia. Several species have been implicated in oral disease.
Staphylococcus	Staphylococcus is a genus of Gram-positive bacteria. Under the microscope they appear round , and form in grape-like clusters. The Staphylococcus genus include just thirty-three species.
Staphylococcus aureus	Staphylococcus aureus is the most common cause of staph infections. It is a spherical bacterium, frequently part of the skin flora found in the nose and on skin. About 20% of the population are long-term carriers of S. aureus.

Go to **Cram101.com** for Interactive Practice Exams for this book or virtually any of your books for $4.95/month.
And, **NEVER** highlight a book again!

Prevotella	Prevotella is a genus of bacteria. "Bacteroides melaninogenicus" has recently been reclassified and split into Prevotella melaninogenica and Prevotella intermedia. Several species have been implicated in oral disease.
Pseudomonas	Pseudomonas is a genus of gamma proteobacteria, belonging to the larger family of pseudomonads. Recently, 16S rRNA sequence analysis has redefined the taxonomy of many bacterial species. As a result the genus Pseudomonas includes strains formerly classified in the genera Chryseomonas and Flavimonas.
Salmonella	Salmonella is a genus of rod-shaped, Gram-negative, non-spore forming, predominantly motile enterobacteria with diameters around 0.7 to 1.5 µm, lengths from 2 to 5 µm, and flagella which project in all directions (i.e. peritrichous.) They are chemoorganotrophs, obtaining their energy from oxidation and reduction reactions using organic sources and are facultative anaerobes; most species produce hydrogen sulfide, which can readily be detected by growing them on media containing ferrous sulfate, such as TSI. Most isolates exist in two phases; phase I is the motile phase and phase II the non-motile phase. Cultures that are non-motile upon primary culture may be swithched to the motile phase using a Craigie tube.
Vibrio	Vibrio is a genus of Gram-negative bacteria possessing a curved rod shape. Typically found in saltwater, Vibrio are facultative anaerobes that test positive for oxidase and do not form spores. All members of the genus are motile and have polar flagella with sheaths.
Vibrio cholerae	Vibrio cholerae is a motile gram negative curved-rod shaped bacterium with a polar flagellum that causes cholera in humans. V. cholerae and other species of the genus Vibrio belong to the gamma subdivision of the Proteobacteria. There are two major strains of V. cholerae, classic and El Tor, and numerous other serogroups.
Pertussis	Pertussis is a highly contagious disease caused by the bacterium Bordetella Pertussis It derived its name from the "whoop" sound made from the inspiration of air after a cough. A similar, milder disease is caused by B. para Pertussis .
Tetanus	Tetanus is a medical condition characterized by a prolonged contraction of skeletal muscle fibers. The primary symptoms are caused by tetanospasmin, a neurotoxin produced by the Gram-positive, obligate anaerobic bacterium Clostridium tetani. Infection generally occurs through wound contamination and often involves a cut or deep puncture wound.
Neisseria	The Neisseria are a large family of commensal bacteria that colonize the mucosal surfaces of many animals. Of the eleven species that colonize humans, only two are pathogens. N. meningitidis and N. gonorrhoeae often cause asymptomatic infections, a commensal-like behavior.
Neisseria meningitidis	Neisseria meningitidis is a heterotrophic gram-negative diplococcal bacterium best known for its role in meningitis and other forms of meningococcal disease such as meningococcemia. N. meningitidis is a major cause of morbidity and mortality in childhood in industrialized countries and is responsible for epidemics in Africa and in Asia.

Go to **Cram101.com** for Interactive Practice Exams for this book or virtually any of your books for $4.95/month.
And, **NEVER** highlight a book again!

Approximately 2500 to 3500 cases of N meningitidis infection occur annually in the United States, with a case rate of about 1 in 100,000.

Tuberculosis	Tuberculosis is a common and often deadly infectious disease caused by mycobacteria, in humans mainly Mycobacterium Tuberculosis . Tuberculosis usually attacks the lungs (as pulmonary TB) but can also affect the central nervous system, the lymphatic system, the circulatory system, the genitourinary system, the gastrointestinal system, bones, joints, and even the skin. Other mycobacteria such as Mycobacterium bovis, Mycobacterium africanum, Mycobacterium canetti, and Mycobacterium microti also cause Tuberculosis, but these species are less common in humans.
Serratia	Serratia is a genus of Gram-negative, facultatively anaerobic, rod-shaped bacteria of the Enterobacteriaceae family. The most common species in the genus, S. marcescens, is normally the only pathogen and usually causes nosocomial infections. However, rare strains of S. plymuthica, S. liquefaciens, S. rubidaea, and S. odoriferae have caused diseases through infection.
Serratia marcescens	Serratia marcescens is a species of Gram-negative, rod-shaped bacteria in the family Enterobacteriaceae. A human pathogen, S. marcescens is involved in nosocomial infections, particularly catheter-associated bacteremia, urinary tract infections and wound infections, and is responsible for 1.4% of nosocomial bacteremia cases in the United States. It is commonly found in the respiratory and urinary tracts of hospitalized adults and in the gastrointestinal system of children.
Staphylococcus	Staphylococcus is a genus of Gram-positive bacteria. Under the microscope they appear round , and form in grape-like clusters. The Staphylococcus genus include just thirty-three species.
Staphylococcus aureus	Staphylococcus aureus is the most common cause of staph infections. It is a spherical bacterium, frequently part of the skin flora found in the nose and on skin. About 20% of the population are long-term carriers of S. aureus.
Salmonella enterica	Salmonella enterica is a rod shaped, flagellated, aerobic, Gram-negative bacterium, and a member of the genus Salmonella. S. enterica has an extraordinarily large number of serovars or strains--up to 2000 have been described. · Salmonella enterica Serovar Typhi (historically elevated to species status as S. typhi) is the disease agent in typhoid fever. The genome sequences of Serovar Typhi has been established. · Salmonella enterica Serovar Typhimurium (also known as S. typhimurium) can lead to a form of human gastroenteritis sometimes referred to as salmonellosis. · The genome sequences of serovar Typhimurium LT2 have been established. Also an analysis of the proteome of Typhimurium LT2 under differing environmental conditions has been performed .

Go to **Cram101.com** for Interactive Practice Exams for this book or virtually any of your books for $4.95/month.
And, **NEVER** highlight a book again!

Salmonella	Salmonella is a genus of rod-shaped, Gram-negative, non-spore forming, predominantly motile enterobacteria with diameters around 0.7 to 1.5 Âµm, lengths from 2 to 5 Âµm, and flagella which project in all directions (i.e. peritrichous.) They are chemoorganotrophs, obtaining their energy from oxidation and reduction reactions using organic sources and are facultative anaerobes; most species produce hydrogen sulfide, which can readily be detected by growing them on media containing ferrous sulfate, such as TSI. Most isolates exist in two phases; phase I is the motile phase and phase II the non-motile phase. Cultures that are non-motile upon primary culture may be swithched to the motile phase using a Craigie tube.
Erwinia	Erwinia is a genus of Enterobacteriaceae bacteria containing mostly plant pathogenic species which was named for the first phytobacteriologist, Erwin Smith. It is a gram negative bacterium related to E.coli, Shigella, Salmonella and Yersinia. It is primarily a rod-shaped bacteria.
Neisseria	The Neisseria are a large family of commensal bacteria that colonize the mucosal surfaces of many animals. Of the eleven species that colonize humans, only two are pathogens. N. meningitidis and N. gonorrhoeae often cause asymptomatic infections, a commensal-like behavior.
Neisseria gonorrhoeae	Neisseria gonorrhoeae or Gonococcus, is a species of Gram-negative kidney bean-shaped diplococci bacteria responsible for the sexually transmitted disease gonorrhoea. N.gonorrhoeae was first described by Albert Neisser in 1879. Neisseria are fastidious cocci, requiring nutrient supplementation to grow in laboratory cultures.
Shigella	Shigella is a genus of Gram-negative, non-spore forming rod-shaped bacteria closely related to Escherichia coli and Salmonella. The causative agent of human shigellosis, Shigella cause disease in primates, but not in other mammals. It is only naturally found in humans and apes.
Pseudomonas	Pseudomonas is a genus of gamma proteobacteria, belonging to the larger family of pseudomonads. Recently, 16S rRNA sequence analysis has redefined the taxonomy of many bacterial species. As a result the genus Pseudomonas includes strains formerly classified in the genera Chryseomonas and Flavimonas.
Tuberculosis	Tuberculosis is a common and often deadly infectious disease caused by mycobacteria, in humans mainly Mycobacterium Tuberculosis . Tuberculosis usually attacks the lungs (as pulmonary TB) but can also affect the central nervous system, the lymphatic system, the circulatory system, the genitourinary system, the gastrointestinal system, bones, joints, and even the skin. Other mycobacteria such as Mycobacterium bovis, Mycobacterium africanum, Mycobacterium canetti, and Mycobacterium microti also cause Tuberculosis, but these species are less common in humans.
Staphylococcus	Staphylococcus is a genus of Gram-positive bacteria. Under the microscope they appear round , and form in grape-like clusters. The Staphylococcus genus include just thirty-three species.

Go to **Cram101.com** for Interactive Practice Exams for this book or virtually any of your books for $4.95/month.
And, **NEVER** highlight a book again!

Staphylococcus aureus	Staphylococcus aureus is the most common cause of staph infections. It is a spherical bacterium, frequently part of the skin flora found in the nose and on skin. About 20% of the population are long-term carriers of S. aureus.
Antiretroviral drugs	Antiretroviral drugs are medications for the treatment of infection by retroviruses, primarily HIV. When several such drugs, typically three or four, are taken in combination, the approach is known as highly active antiretroviral therapy, or HAART. The American National Institutes of Health and other organizations recommend offering antiretroviral treatment to all patients with AIDS. Because of the complexity of selecting and following a regimen, the severity of the side-effects and the importance of compliance to prevent viral resistance. However, such organizations emphasize the importance of involving patients in therapy choices, and recommend analyzing the risks and the potential benefits to patients without symptoms. There are different classes of Antiretroviral drugs that act at different stages of the HIV life-cycle.
Reverse transcriptase inhibitors	Reverse transcriptase inhibitors (Reverse transcriptase inhibitorss) are a class of antiretroviral drug used to treat HIV infection, tumors, and cancer. Reverse transcriptase inhibitorss inhibit activity of reverse transcriptase, a viral DNA polymerase enzyme that retroviruses need to reproduce. When HIV infects a cell, reverse transcriptase copies the viral single stranded RNA genome into a double-stranded viral DNA. The viral DNA is then integrated into the host chromosomal DNA, which then allows host cellular processes, such as transcription and translation to reproduce the virus.

Go to **Cram101.com** for Interactive Practice Exams for this book or virtually any of your books for $4.95/month.
And, **NEVER** highlight a book again!

Neisseria	The Neisseria are a large family of commensal bacteria that colonize the mucosal surfaces of many animals. Of the eleven species that colonize humans, only two are pathogens. N. meningitidis and N. gonorrhoeae often cause asymptomatic infections, a commensal-like behavior.
Neisseria gonorrhoeae	Neisseria gonorrhoeae or Gonococcus, is a species of Gram-negative kidney bean-shaped diplococci bacteria responsible for the sexually transmitted disease gonorrhoea. N.gonorrhoeae was first described by Albert Neisser in 1879. Neisseria are fastidious cocci, requiring nutrient supplementation to grow in laboratory cultures.
Sulfolobus	In taxonomy, Sulfolobus is a genus of the Sulfolobaceae. Sulfolobus species grow in volcanic springs with optimal growth occurring at pH 2-3 and temperatures of 75-80 °C, making them acidophiles and thermophiles respectively. Sulfolobus cells are irregularly shaped and flagellar.
Streptobacillus	Streptobacillus is a genus of aerobic, gram-negative facultative anaerobe bacteria, which grow in culture as rods in chains. Species associated with infection - S. moniliformis Reported susceptibilities and therapies - penicillin, erythromycin Associated infections: the Haverhill fever form of rat bite fever. (Notes Spirillum minus is also an agent of rat bite fever, in the form known as sodoku.)
Pseudomonas	Pseudomonas is a genus of gamma proteobacteria, belonging to the larger family of pseudomonads. Recently, 16S rRNA sequence analysis has redefined the taxonomy of many bacterial species. As a result the genus Pseudomonas includes strains formerly classified in the genera Chryseomonas and Flavimonas.
Cephalosporin	The Cephalosporins (IPA: /ˌsɛfəˈlɔːspɔːrɪn/) are a class of β-lactam antibiotics originally derived from Acremonium, which was previously known as "Cephalosporium". Together with cephamycins they constitute a subgroup of β-lactam antibiotics called cephems. Cephalosporin compounds were first isolated from cultures of Cephalosporium acremonium from a sewer in Sardinia in 1948 by Italian scientist Giuseppe Brotzu .
Prevotella	Prevotella is a genus of bacteria. "Bacteroides melaninogenicus" has recently been reclassified and split into Prevotella melaninogenica and Prevotella intermedia. Several species have been implicated in oral disease.
Carbapenem	Carbapenems are a class of beta-lactam antibiotics with a broad spectrum of antibacterial activity. They have a structure that renders them highly resistant to beta-lactamases. Carbapenem antibiotics were originally developed from thienamycin, a naturally-derived product of Streptomyces cattleya.
Imipenem	Imipenem is an intravenous β-lactam antibiotic developed in 1985. It has an extremely broad spectrum of activity. Imipenem belongs to the subgroup of carbapenems.

Go to **Cram101.com** for Interactive Practice Exams for this book or virtually any of your books for $4.95/month.
And, **NEVER** highlight a book again!

Rickettsiales	The Rickettsiales are an order of small proteobacteria. Most of those described survive only as endosymbionts of other cells. Some are notable pathogens, including Rickettsia, which causes a variety of diseases in humans.
Staphylococcus	Staphylococcus is a genus of Gram-positive bacteria. Under the microscope they appear round , and form in grape-like clusters. The Staphylococcus genus include just thirty-three species.
Staphylococcus aureus	Staphylococcus aureus is the most common cause of staph infections. It is a spherical bacterium, frequently part of the skin flora found in the nose and on skin. About 20% of the population are long-term carriers of S. aureus.
Cefaclor	Cefaclor is a second-generation cephalosporin antibiotic used to treat certain infections caused by bacteria such as pneumonia and ear, lung, skin, throat, and urinary tract infections. Cefaclor belongs to the family of antibiotics known as the cephalosporins. The cephalosporins are broad-spectrum antibiotics that are used for the treatment of septicaemia, pneumonia, meningitis, biliary-tract infections, peritonitis, and urinary-tract infections.
Cefamandole	Cefamandole is a second-generation broad-spectrum cephalosporin antibiotic. The clinically used form of Cefamandole is the formate ester Cefamandole nafate, a prodrug which is administered parenterally. Cefamandole is no longer available in the United States.
Tuberculosis	Tuberculosis is a common and often deadly infectious disease caused by mycobacteria, in humans mainly Mycobacterium Tuberculosis . Tuberculosis usually attacks the lungs (as pulmonary TB) but can also affect the central nervous system, the lymphatic system, the circulatory system, the genitourinary system, the gastrointestinal system, bones, joints, and even the skin. Other mycobacteria such as Mycobacterium bovis, Mycobacterium africanum, Mycobacterium canetti, and Mycobacterium microti also cause Tuberculosis, but these species are less common in humans.
Vancomycin-resistant	Vancomycin-resistant enterococcus (VRE) is the name given to a group of bacterial species of the genus Enterococcus that is resistant to the antibiotic vancomycin. Enterococci are enteric and can be found in the digestive and urinary tracts of some humans. VRE was discovered in 1985 and is particularly dangerous to immunocompromised individuals.
Vancomycin-resistant Staphylococcus aureus	Vancomycin-resistant Staphylococcus aureus is a strain of Staphylococcus aureus that has become resistant to the glycopeptide antibiotic vancomycin. With the increase of staphylococcal resistance to methicillin, vancomycin (or another antibiotic teicoplanin) is often a treatment of choice in infections with methicillin-resistant Staphylococcus aureus (MRSA.) Vancomycin resistance is still a rare occurrence.

Go to **Cram101.com** for Interactive Practice Exams for this book or virtually any of your books for $4.95/month.
And, **NEVER** highlight a book again!

Rickettsia	Rickettsia is a genus of motile, Gram-negative, non-sporeforming, highly pleomorphic bacteria that can present as cocci (0.1 μm in diameter), rods (1-4 μm long) or thread-like (10 μm long.) Obligate intracellular parasites, the Rickettsia survival depends on entry, growth, and replication within the cytoplasm of eukaryotic host cells (typically endothelial cells.) Because of this, Rickettsia cannot live in artificial nutrient environments and are grown either in tissue or embryo cultures (typically, chicken embryos are used.)
Typhus	Typhus is any of several similar diseases caused by Rickettsiae. The name comes from the Greek typhos meaning smoky or hazy,describing the state of mind of those affected with Typhus. The causative organism Rickettsia is an obligate parasite and cannot survive for long outside living cells.
Azithromycin	Azithromycin is an azalide, a subclass of macrolide antibiotics. Azithromycin with brand names AZORTA from Dr. Reddy"s (FGP) IN PHARYNGITIS ' TONSILITIS (INDIA) APO-Azithromycin in Canada; Zithromax in Finland, Italy, The United Kingdom, The United States, Australia, Portugal, South Africa, Canada, Thailand and Belgium; Zithromac in Japan; Vinzam / Zitromax in Spain; Zmax; Sumamed in Croatia; ATM, Aztrin,Azigard,Zitrocin, Azibiot, Azifine, AziCip, Azi Sandoz, Aziswift in India, Azocam and Bactizith in Pakistan) is one of the world"s best-selling antibiotics, and is derived from erythromycin; however, it differs chemically from erythromycin in that a methyl-substituted nitrogen atom is incorporated into the lactone ring, thus making the lactone ring 15-membered. Azithromycin is used to treat or prevent certain bacterial infections, most often those causing middle ear infections, tonsillitis, throat infections, laryngitis, bronchitis, pneumonia, Typhoid, yeast infections, and sinusitis.
Clarithromycin	Clarithromycin is a macrolide antibiotic used to treat pharyngitis, tonsillitis, acute maxillary sinusitis, acute bacterial exacerbation of chronic bronchitis, pneumonia (especially atypical pneumonias associated with Chlamydia pneumoniae or TWAR), skin and skin structure infections, and, in HIV and AIDS patients to prevent, and to treat, disseminated Mycobacterium avium complex (MAC). In addition, it is sometimes used to treat Legionellosis and lyme disease. Clarithromycin is available under several brand names, for example Crixan, Biaxin, Klaricid, Klabax, Claripen, Claridar, Fromilid, Clacid, Vikrol, and infex.
Erythromycin	Erythromycin is a macrolide antibiotic that has an antimicrobial spectrum similar to or slightly wider than that of penicillin, and is often used for people who have an allergy to penicillins. For respiratory tract infections, it has better coverage of atypical organisms, including mycoplasma and Legionellosis. It was first marketed by Eli Lilly and Company, and it is today commonly known as EES (Erythromycin ethylsuccinate, an ester prodrug that is commonly administered).
Ketolides	Ketolides are antibiotics belonging to the macrolide group. Ketolides are derived from erythromycin by substituting the cladinose sugar with a keto-group and attaching a cyclic carbamate group in the lactone ring. These modifications give Ketolides much broader spectrum than other macrolides.
Telithromycin	Telithromycin is the first ketolide antibiotic to enter clinical use. It is used to treat mild to moderate respiratory infections. Telithromycin is sold under the brand name of Ketek.

Go to **Cram101.com** for Interactive Practice Exams for this book or virtually any of your books for $4.95/month.
And, **NEVER** highlight a book again!

Shigella	Shigella is a genus of Gram-negative, non-spore forming rod-shaped bacteria closely related to Escherichia coli and Salmonella. The causative agent of human shigellosis, Shigella cause disease in primates, but not in other mammals. It is only naturally found in humans and apes.
Yersinia	Yersinia is a genus of bacteria in the family Enterobacteriaceae. Yersinia are Gram-negative rod shaped bacteria, a few micrometers long and fractions of a micrometer in diameter, and are facultative anaerobes. Some members of Yersinia are pathogenic in humans.
Gatifloxacin	Gatifloxacin sold under the brand names Gatiflo, Tequin and Zymar, is an antibiotic of the fourth-generation fluoroquinolone family, that like other members of that family, inhibits the bacterial enzymes DNA gyrase and topoisomerase IV. Bristol-Myers Squibb introduced Gatifloxacin in 1999 under the proprietary name Tequin for the treatment of respiratory tract infections, having licensed the medication from Kyorin Pharmaceutical Company of Japan. Allergan produces an eye-drop formulation called Zymar. In many countries, Gatifloxacin is also available as tablets and in various aqueous solutions for intravenous therapy.
Gemifloxacin	Gemifloxacin mesylate (trade name Factive, Oscient Pharmaceuticals) is an oral broad-spectrum quinolone antibacterial agent used in the treatment of acute bacterial exacerbation of chronic bronchitis and mild-to-moderate pneumonia. Oscient Pharmaceuticals has licensed the active ingredient from LG Life Sciences of Korea. Gemifloxacin is indicated for the treatment of infections caused by susceptible strains of the designated microorganisms in the conditions listed below.
Norfloxacin	Norfloxacin is a synthetic chemotherapeutic agent occasionally used to treat common as well as complicated urinary tract infections. It is sold under various brand names with the most common being Noroxin. In form of ophthalmic solutions it is known as Chibroxin.
Salt	Salt played a major role during the Civil War. Salt not only preserved food in the days before refrigeration, but was also vital in the curing of leather. Union general William Tecumseh Sherman once said that "Salt is eminently contraband", as an army that has Salt can adequately feed its men.
Yersinia pestis	Yersinia pestis is a Gram-negative rod-shaped bacterium belonging to the family Enterobacteriaceae. It is a facultative anaerobe that can infect humans and other animals. Human Y. pestis infection takes three main forms: pneumonic, septicemic, and the notorious bubonic plagues.
Antiretroviral drugs	Antiretroviral drugs are medications for the treatment of infection by retroviruses, primarily HIV. When several such drugs, typically three or four, are taken in combination, the approach is known as highly active antiretroviral therapy, or HAART. The American National Institutes of Health and other organizations recommend offering antiretroviral treatment to all patients with AIDS. Because of the complexity of selecting and following a regimen, the severity of the side-effects and the importance of compliance to prevent viral resistance. However, such organizations emphasize the importance of involving patients in therapy choices, and recommend analyzing the risks and the potential benefits to patients without symptoms.

Go to **Cram101.com** for Interactive Practice Exams for this book or virtually any of your books for $4.95/month.
And, **NEVER** highlight a book again!

There are different classes of Antiretroviral drugs that act at different stages of the HIV life-cycle.

Phage therapy

Phage therapy is the therapeutic use of bacteriophages to treat pathogenic bacterial infections. Although extensively used and developed mainly in former Soviet Union countries for about 90 years, this method of therapy is still being tested elsewhere for treatment of a variety of bacterial and poly-microbial biofilm infections, and has not yet been approved in countries other than Georgia. Phage therapy has many potential applications in human medicine as well as dentistry, veterinary science, and agriculture.

Go to **Cram101.com** for Interactive Practice Exams for this book or virtually any of your books for $4.95/month.
And, **NEVER** highlight a book again!

Pseudomonas	Pseudomonas is a genus of gamma proteobacteria, belonging to the larger family of pseudomonads. Recently, 16S rRNA sequence analysis has redefined the taxonomy of many bacterial species. As a result the genus Pseudomonas includes strains formerly classified in the genera Chryseomonas and Flavimonas.
Staphylococcus	Staphylococcus is a genus of Gram-positive bacteria. Under the microscope they appear round , and form in grape-like clusters. The Staphylococcus genus include just thirty-three species.
Staphylococcus aureus	Staphylococcus aureus is the most common cause of staph infections. It is a spherical bacterium, frequently part of the skin flora found in the nose and on skin. About 20% of the population are long-term carriers of S. aureus.
Thermotoga	Thermotoga are thermophile or hyperthermophile bacteria whose cell is wrapped in an outer "toga" membrane. They were named by microbiologist Karl Stetter. They metabolize carbohydrates.
Veillonella	Veillonella are gram-negative anaerobic cocci. This bacterium is well known for its lactate fermenting abilities. They are a normal bacterium in the intestines and oral mucosa of mammals.
Neisseria	The Neisseria are a large family of commensal bacteria that colonize the mucosal surfaces of many animals. Of the eleven species that colonize humans, only two are pathogens. N. meningitidis and N. gonorrhoeae often cause asymptomatic infections, a commensal-like behavior.
Neisseria gonorrhoeae	Neisseria gonorrhoeae or Gonococcus, is a species of Gram-negative kidney bean-shaped diplococci bacteria responsible for the sexually transmitted disease gonorrhoea. N.gonorrhoeae was first described by Albert Neisser in 1879. Neisseria are fastidious cocci, requiring nutrient supplementation to grow in laboratory cultures.
Streptobacillus	Streptobacillus is a genus of aerobic, gram-negative facultative anaerobe bacteria, which grow in culture as rods in chains. Species associated with infection - S. moniliformis Reported susceptibilities and therapies - penicillin, erythromycin Associated infections: the Haverhill fever form of rat bite fever. (Notes Spirillum minus is also an agent of rat bite fever, in the form known as sodoku.)
Salt	Salt played a major role during the Civil War. Salt not only preserved food in the days before refrigeration, but was also vital in the curing of leather. Union general William Tecumseh Sherman once said that "Salt is eminently contraband", as an army that has Salt can adequately feed its men.

Go to **Cram101.com** for Interactive Practice Exams for this book or virtually any of your books for $4.95/month.
And, **NEVER** highlight a book again!

Shiga toxin	Shiga toxin s are a family of related toxins with two major groups, Stx1 and Stx2, whose genes are considered to be part of the genome of lambdoid prophages. The toxins are named for Kiyoshi Shiga, who first described the bacterial origin of dysentery caused by Shigella dysenteriae. The most common sources for Shiga toxin are the bacteria S. dysenteriae and the Shigatoxigenic group of Escherichia coli (Shiga toxin EC), which includes serotype O157:H7 and other enterohemorrhagic E. coli.
Erwinia	Erwinia is a genus of Enterobacteriaceae bacteria containing mostly plant pathogenic species which was named for the first phytobacteriologist, Erwin Smith. It is a gram negative bacterium related to E.coli, Shigella, Salmonella and Yersinia. It is primarily a rod-shaped bacteria.
Necrotizing fasciitis	Necrotizing fasciitis , commonly known as flesh-eating disease or flesh-eating bacteria, is a rare infection of the deeper layers of skin and subcutaneous tissues, easily spreading across the fascial plane within the subcutaneous tissue. Type I describes a polymicrobial infection, whereas Type II describes a monomicrobial infection. Many types of bacteria can cause Necrotizing fasciitis (eg.
Shigella	Shigella is a genus of Gram-negative, non-spore forming rod-shaped bacteria closely related to Escherichia coli and Salmonella. The causative agent of human shigellosis, Shigella cause disease in primates, but not in other mammals. It is only naturally found in humans and apes.

Go to **Cram101.com** for Interactive Practice Exams for this book or virtually any of your books for $4.95/month.
And, **NEVER** highlight a book again!

Neisseria	The Neisseria are a large family of commensal bacteria that colonize the mucosal surfaces of many animals. Of the eleven species that colonize humans, only two are pathogens. N. meningitidis and N. gonorrhoeae often cause asymptomatic infections, a commensal-like behavior.
Neisseria gonorrhoeae	Neisseria gonorrhoeae or Gonococcus, is a species of Gram-negative kidney bean-shaped diplococci bacteria responsible for the sexually transmitted disease gonorrhoea. N.gonorrhoeae was first described by Albert Neisser in 1879. Neisseria are fastidious cocci, requiring nutrient supplementation to grow in laboratory cultures.
Neisseria meningitidis	Neisseria meningitidis is a heterotrophic gram-negative diplococcal bacterium best known for its role in meningitis and other forms of meningococcal disease such as meningococcemia. N. meningitidis is a major cause of morbidity and mortality in childhood in industrialized countries and is responsible for epidemics in Africa and in Asia. Approximately 2500 to 3500 cases of N meningitidis infection occur annually in the United States, with a case rate of about 1 in 100,000.
Planctomycetes	Planctomycetes are a phylum of aquatic bacteria and are found in field samples of brackish, and marine and fresh water samples. They reproduce by budding. In structure, the organisms of this group are ovoid and have a holdfast, called the stalk, at the nonreproductive end that helps them to attach to each other during budding.
Staphylococcus	Staphylococcus is a genus of Gram-positive bacteria. Under the microscope they appear round , and form in grape-like clusters. The Staphylococcus genus include just thirty-three species.
Staphylococcus aureus	Staphylococcus aureus is the most common cause of staph infections. It is a spherical bacterium, frequently part of the skin flora found in the nose and on skin. About 20% of the population are long-term carriers of S. aureus.
Pseudomonas	Pseudomonas is a genus of gamma proteobacteria, belonging to the larger family of pseudomonads. Recently, 16S rRNA sequence analysis has redefined the taxonomy of many bacterial species. As a result the genus Pseudomonas includes strains formerly classified in the genera Chryseomonas and Flavimonas.
Salmonella	Salmonella is a genus of rod-shaped, Gram-negative, non-spore forming, predominantly motile enterobacteria with diameters around 0.7 to 1.5 µm, lengths from 2 to 5 µm, and flagella which project in all directions (i.e. peritrichous.) They are chemoorganotrophs, obtaining their energy from oxidation and reduction reactions using organic sources and are facultative anaerobes; most species produce hydrogen sulfide, which can readily be detected by growing them on media containing ferrous sulfate, such as TSI. Most isolates exist in two phases; phase I is the motile phase and phase II the non-motile phase. Cultures that are non-motile upon primary culture may be swithched to the motile phase using a Craigie tube.

Go to **Cram101.com** for Interactive Practice Exams for this book or virtually any of your books for $4.95/month.
And, **NEVER** highlight a book again!

Tetanus

Tetanus is a medical condition characterized by a prolonged contraction of skeletal muscle fibers. The primary symptoms are caused by tetanospasmin, a neurotoxin produced by the Gram-positive, obligate anaerobic bacterium Clostridium tetani. Infection generally occurs through wound contamination and often involves a cut or deep puncture wound.

Rickettsiales

The Rickettsiales are an order of small proteobacteria. Most of those described survive only as endosymbionts of other cells. Some are notable pathogens, including Rickettsia, which causes a variety of diseases in humans.

Sulfolobus

In taxonomy, Sulfolobus is a genus of the Sulfolobaceae.
Sulfolobus species grow in volcanic springs with optimal growth occurring at pH 2-3 and temperatures of 75-80 °C, making them acidophiles and thermophiles respectively. Sulfolobus cells are irregularly shaped and flagellar.

Prevotella

Prevotella is a genus of bacteria.
"Bacteroides melaninogenicus" has recently been reclassified and split into Prevotella melaninogenica and Prevotella intermedia.
Several species have been implicated in oral disease.

Go to **Cram101.com** for Interactive Practice Exams for this book or virtually any of your books for $4.95/month.
And, **NEVER** highlight a book again!

Shigella	Shigella is a genus of Gram-negative, non-spore forming rod-shaped bacteria closely related to Escherichia coli and Salmonella. The causative agent of human shigellosis, Shigella cause disease in primates, but not in other mammals. It is only naturally found in humans and apes.
Staphylococcus	Staphylococcus is a genus of Gram-positive bacteria. Under the microscope they appear round , and form in grape-like clusters. The Staphylococcus genus include just thirty-three species.
Staphylococcus aureus	Staphylococcus aureus is the most common cause of staph infections. It is a spherical bacterium, frequently part of the skin flora found in the nose and on skin. About 20% of the population are long-term carriers of S. aureus.
Neisseria	The Neisseria are a large family of commensal bacteria that colonize the mucosal surfaces of many animals. Of the eleven species that colonize humans, only two are pathogens. N. meningitidis and N. gonorrhoeae often cause asymptomatic infections, a commensal-like behavior.
Neisseria meningitidis	Neisseria meningitidis is a heterotrophic gram-negative diplococcal bacterium best known for its role in meningitis and other forms of meningococcal disease such as meningococcemia. N. meningitidis is a major cause of morbidity and mortality in childhood in industrialized countries and is responsible for epidemics in Africa and in Asia. Approximately 2500 to 3500 cases of N meningitidis infection occur annually in the United States, with a case rate of about 1 in 100,000.
Salt	Salt played a major role during the Civil War. Salt not only preserved food in the days before refrigeration, but was also vital in the curing of leather. Union general William Tecumseh Sherman once said that "Salt is eminently contraband", as an army that has Salt can adequately feed its men.
Serratia	Serratia is a genus of Gram-negative, facultatively anaerobic, rod-shaped bacteria of the Enterobacteriaceae family. The most common species in the genus, S. marcescens, is normally the only pathogen and usually causes nosocomial infections. However, rare strains of S. plymuthica, S. liquefaciens, S. rubidaea, and S. odoriferae have caused diseases through infection.
Serratia marcescens	Serratia marcescens is a species of Gram-negative, rod-shaped bacteria in the family Enterobacteriaceae. A human pathogen, S. marcescens is involved in nosocomial infections, particularly catheter-associated bacteremia, urinary tract infections and wound infections, and is responsible for 1.4% of nosocomial bacteremia cases in the United States. It is commonly found in the respiratory and urinary tracts of hospitalized adults and in the gastrointestinal system of children.
Vancomycin-resistant	Vancomycin-resistant enterococcus (VRE) is the name given to a group of bacterial species of the genus Enterococcus that is resistant to the antibiotic vancomycin. Enterococci are enteric and can be found in the digestive and urinary tracts of some humans. VRE was discovered in 1985 and is particularly dangerous to immunocompromised individuals.

Go to **Cram101.com** for Interactive Practice Exams for this book or virtually any of your books for $4.95/month.
And, **NEVER** highlight a book again!

Shiga toxin	Shiga toxin s are a family of related toxins with two major groups, Stx1 and Stx2, whose genes are considered to be part of the genome of lambdoid prophages. The toxins are named for Kiyoshi Shiga, who first described the bacterial origin of dysentery caused by Shigella dysenteriae. The most common sources for Shiga toxin are the bacteria S. dysenteriae and the Shigatoxigenic group of Escherichia coli (Shiga toxin EC), which includes serotype O157:H7 and other enterohemorrhagic E. coli.
Rheumatic fever	Rheumatic fever is an inflammatory disease that may develop two to three weeks after a Group A streptococcal infection (such as strep throat or scarlet fever.) It is believed to be caused by antibody cross-reactivity and can involve the heart, joints, skin, and brain. Acute Rheumatic fever commonly appears in children ages 5 through 15, with only 20% of first time attacks occurring in adults.
Tularemia	Tularemia is a serious infectious disease caused by the bacterium Francisella tularensis. A gram-negative, non-motile coccobacillus, the bacterium has several subspecies with varying degrees of virulence. The most important of those is F. tularensis tularensis (Type A), which is found in lagomorphs in North America and is highly virulent for humans and domestic rabbits.
Bacillus anthracis	Bacillus anthracis is a Gram-positive spore-forming, rod-shaped bacterium, with a width of 1-1.2Âµm and a length of 3-5Âµm. It can be grown in an ordinary nutrient medium under aerobic or anaerobic conditions. It is the only bacterium with a protein capsule (D-glutamate), and the only pathogenic bacteria to carry its own adenylyl cyclase virulence factor (edema factor).
Yersinia	Yersinia is a genus of bacteria in the family Enterobacteriaceae. Yersinia are Gram-negative rod shaped bacteria, a few micrometers long and fractions of a micrometer in diameter, and are facultative anaerobes. Some members of Yersinia are pathogenic in humans.
Spirillum	Spirillum in microbiology refers to a bacterium with a cell body that twists like a spiral. It is the third distinct bacterial cell shape type besides coccus and bacillus cells. Spirillum is a genus of gram-negative bacteria.
Streptobacillus	Streptobacillus is a genus of aerobic, gram-negative facultative anaerobe bacteria, which grow in culture as rods in chains. Species associated with infection - S. moniliformis Reported susceptibilities and therapies - penicillin, erythromycin Associated infections: the Haverhill fever form of rat bite fever. (Notes Spirillum minus is also an agent of rat bite fever, in the form known as sodoku.)
Plague	Plague is a deadly infectious disease caused by the enterobacteria Yersinia pestis (Pasteurella pestis.) Plague is a zoonotic, primarily carried by rodents (most notably rats) and spread to humans via fleas. Plague is notorious throughout history, due to the unprecedented scale of death and devastation it brought.

Go to **Cram101.com** for Interactive Practice Exams for this book or virtually any of your books for $4.95/month.
And, **NEVER** highlight a book again!

Pneumonic plague	Pneumonic plague is the second most virulent and second least common form of plague (after scepticemic plague), caused by the bacterium Yersinia pestis. Typically, pneumonic form is due to a secondary spread from advanced infection of an initial bubonic form. Primary Pneumonic plague results from inhalation of aerosolized infective droplets and can be transmitted from human to human without involvement of fleas or animals.
Septicemic plague	Septicemic (or septicaemic) plague is a deadly blood infection by yersinia pestis, a gram-negative bacterium. The disease can result from bubonic and pneumonic plague when bacteria enter the blood from the lymphatic and respiratory systems, respectively. Like other forms of gram-negative sepsis, Septicemic plague can cause disseminated intravascular coagulation (DIC), and is almost always fatal.
Sodoku	Sodoku is a bacterial zoonotic disease. It is caused by outnumbered spirochaete Spirillum minus. It is a form of rat-bite fever (RBF.)
Relapsing fever	Relapsing fever is an infection caused by certain bacteria in the genus Borrelia. It is a vector-borne disease that is transmitted through louse or soft-bodied tick bites. Borrelia recurrentis is the only agent of louse-borne disease.
Rickettsia	Rickettsia is a genus of motile, Gram-negative, non-sporeforming, highly pleomorphic bacteria that can present as cocci (0.1 µm in diameter), rods (1-4 µm long) or thread-like (10 µm long.) Obligate intracellular parasites, the Rickettsia survival depends on entry, growth, and replication within the cytoplasm of eukaryotic host cells (typically endothelial cells.) Because of this, Rickettsia cannot live in artificial nutrient environments and are grown either in tissue or embryo cultures (typically, chicken embryos are used.)
Rickettsia prowazekii	Rickettsia prowazekii is a species of gram negative, bacillus, obligate intracellular parasitic, aerobic bacteria that is the etiologic agent of epidemic typhus, transmitted in the feces of lice and fleas. In North America, the main reservoir for R. prowazekii is the flying squirrel. R. prowazekii is often surrounded by a protein microcapsular layer and slime layer; the natural life cycle of the bacterium generally involves a vertebrate and an invertebrate host, usually an arthropod, typically a louse.
Typhus	Typhus is any of several similar diseases caused by Rickettsiae. The name comes from the Greek typhos meaning smoky or hazy, describing the state of mind of those affected with Typhus. The causative organism Rickettsia is an obligate parasite and cannot survive for long outside living cells.
Rocky Mountain spotted fever	Rocky Mountain spotted fever is the most lethal and most frequently reported rickettsial illness in the United States. It has been diagnosed throughout the Americas. Some synonyms for Rocky Mountain spotted fever in other countries include "tick typhus," "Tobia fever" (Colombia), "São Paulo fever" or "febre maculosa" (Brazil), and "fiebre manchada" (Mexico.)
Neisseria gonorrhoeae	Neisseria gonorrhoeae or Gonococcus, is a species of Gram-negative kidney bean-shaped diplococci bacteria responsible for the sexually transmitted disease gonorrhoea. N.gonorrhoeae was first described by Albert Neisser in 1879.

Go to **Cram101.com** for Interactive Practice Exams for this book or virtually any of your books for $4.95/month.
And, **NEVER** highlight a book again!

Neisseria are fastidious cocci, requiring nutrient supplementation to grow in laboratory cultures.

Go to **Cram101.com** for Interactive Practice Exams for this book or virtually any of your books for $4.95/month.
And, **NEVER** highlight a book again!

RecA	RecA is a 38 kilodalton Escherichia coli protein essential for the repair and maintenance of DNA. RecA has a structural and functional homolog in every species in which it has been seriously sought and serves as an archetype for this class of homologous DNA repair proteins. The homologous protein in Homo sapiens is called RAD51.
	RecA has multiple activities, all related to DNA repair.
Streptobacillus	Streptobacillus is a genus of aerobic, gram-negative facultative anaerobe bacteria, which grow in culture as rods in chains.
	Species associated with infection - S. moniliformis
	Reported susceptibilities and therapies - penicillin, erythromycin
	Associated infections: the Haverhill fever form of rat bite fever. (Notes Spirillum minus is also an agent of rat bite fever, in the form known as sodoku.)
Scarlet fever	Scarlet fever is a disease caused by an erythrogenic exotoxin released by Streptococcus pyogenes. The term Scarlatina may be used interchangeably with Scarlet fever, though it is commonly used to indicate the less acute form of Scarlet fever that is often seen since the beginning of the twentieth century.
	It is characterized by:
	· Sore throat
	· Fever
	· Bright red tongue with a "strawberry" appearance
	· Characteristic rash, which:
	· is fine, red, and rough-textured; it blanches upon pressure
	· appears 12-48 hours after the fever
	· generally starts on the chest, armpits, and behind the ears
	· spares the face
	· is worse in the skin folds. These are called Pastia lines (where the rash runs together in the arm pits and groins) appear and can persist after the rash is gone
	· may spread to cover the uvula.
	· The rash begins to fade three to four days after onset and desquamation (peeling) begins. "This phase begins with flakes peeling from the face.
Streptococcal pharyngitis	Streptococcal pharyngitis or streptococcal sore throat is a form of group A streptococcal infection that affects the pharynx and possibly the larynx and tonsils.
	Streptococcal pharyngitis usually appears suddenly with a severe sore throat that may make talking or swallowing painful.
	Signs and symptoms may include

Go to **Cram101.com** for Interactive Practice Exams for this book or virtually any of your books for $4.95/month.
And, **NEVER** highlight a book again!

· Inflamed tonsils
· White spots on the tonsils
· Difficulty swallowing
· Tender cervical lymphadenopathy
· Fever
· Headache (often prior to other symptoms)
· Malaise, general discomfort, feeling ill or uneasy
· Halitosis
· Abdominal pain, nausea and vomiting
· Rash
· Hives
· Chills
· Loss of appetite
· Ear pain
· Peeling of skin on hands and feet

Additional symptoms such as sinusitis, vaginitis, or impetigo may be present if the strep bacteria infects both the throat and a secondary location. For additional information on non-pharynx symptoms, see Group A Streptococcal (GAS) Infection.

Staphylococcus	Staphylococcus is a genus of Gram-positive bacteria. Under the microscope they appear round , and form in grape-like clusters. The Staphylococcus genus include just thirty-three species.
Staphylococcus aureus	Staphylococcus aureus is the most common cause of staph infections. It is a spherical bacterium, frequently part of the skin flora found in the nose and on skin. About 20% of the population are long-term carriers of S. aureus.
Pertussis	Pertussis is a highly contagious disease caused by the bacterium Bordetella Pertussis It derived its name from the "whoop" sound made from the inspiration of air after a cough. A similar, milder disease is caused by B. para Pertussis .
Tuberculosis	Tuberculosis is a common and often deadly infectious disease caused by mycobacteria, in humans mainly Mycobacterium Tuberculosis . Tuberculosis usually attacks the lungs (as pulmonary TB) but can also affect the central nervous system, the lymphatic system, the circulatory system, the genitourinary system, the gastrointestinal system, bones, joints, and even the skin. Other mycobacteria such as Mycobacterium bovis, Mycobacterium africanum, Mycobacterium canetti, and Mycobacterium microti also cause Tuberculosis, but these species are less common in humans.
Rickettsiales	The Rickettsiales are an order of small proteobacteria. Most of those described survive only as endosymbionts of other cells. Some are notable pathogens, including Rickettsia, which causes a variety of diseases in humans.

Go to **Cram101.com** for Interactive Practice Exams for this book or virtually any of your books for $4.95/month.
And, **NEVER** highlight a book again!

Q fever	Q fever is a disease caused by infection with Coxiella burnetii, a bacterium that affects both humans and animals. This organism is uncommon but may be found in cattle, sheep, goats and other domestic mammals, including cats and dogs. The infection results from inhalation of contaminated particles in the air, and from contact with the milk, urine, feces, vaginal mucus, or semen of infected animals.
Psittacosis	In medicine, Psittacosis -- also known as parrot disease, parrot fever, and ornithosis -- is a zoonotic infectious disease caused by a bacterium called Chlamydophila psittaci and contracted not only from parrots, such as macaws, cockatiels and budgerigars, but also from pigeons, sparrows, ducks, hens, gulls and many other species of bird. The incidence of infection in canaries and finches is believed to be lower than in psittacine birds. The word "ornithosis" is only a synonym for "Psittacosis" in certain contexts : more generally the term is applied to any infection that is spread by birds.
Salmonella	Salmonella is a genus of rod-shaped, Gram-negative, non-spore forming, predominantly motile enterobacteria with diameters around 0.7 to 1.5 Âμm, lengths from 2 to 5 Âμm, and flagella which project in all directions (i.e. peritrichous.) They are chemoorganotrophs, obtaining their energy from oxidation and reduction reactions using organic sources and are facultative anaerobes; most species produce hydrogen sulfide, which can readily be detected by growing them on media containing ferrous sulfate, such as TSI. Most isolates exist in two phases; phase I is the motile phase and phase II the non-motile phase. Cultures that are non-motile upon primary culture may be swithched to the motile phase using a Craigie tube.
Paenibacillus	Paenibacillus is a genus of bacteria, originally included within Bacillus. The name reflects this fact: Latin paene means almost, and so the Paenibacilli are literally almost Bacilli. The genus includes P. larvae, which causes American foulbrood in honeybees.

Go to **Cram101.com** for Interactive Practice Exams for this book or virtually any of your books for $4.95/month.
And, **NEVER** highlight a book again!

Prevotella	Prevotella is a genus of bacteria. "Bacteroides melaninogenicus" has recently been reclassified and split into Prevotella melaninogenica and Prevotella intermedia. Several species have been implicated in oral disease.
Oral rehydration therapy	Oral rehydration therapy is a simple, cheap, and effective treatment for dehydration associated with diarrhea, particularly gastroenteritis, such as that caused by cholera or rotavirus. Oral rehydration therapy consists of a solution of salts and sugars which is taken by mouth. It is used around the world, but is most important in the developing world, where it saves millions of children a year from death due to diarrhea--the second leading cause of death in children under five.
Staphylococcus	Staphylococcus is a genus of Gram-positive bacteria. Under the microscope they appear round , and form in grape-like clusters. The Staphylococcus genus include just thirty-three species.
Staphylococcus aureus	Staphylococcus aureus is the most common cause of staph infections. It is a spherical bacterium, frequently part of the skin flora found in the nose and on skin. About 20% of the population are long-term carriers of S. aureus.
Salmonella	Salmonella is a genus of rod-shaped, Gram-negative, non-spore forming, predominantly motile enterobacteria with diameters around 0.7 to 1.5 µm, lengths from 2 to 5 µm, and flagella which project in all directions (i.e. peritrichous.) They are chemoorganotrophs, obtaining their energy from oxidation and reduction reactions using organic sources and are facultative anaerobes; most species produce hydrogen sulfide, which can readily be detected by growing them on media containing ferrous sulfate, such as TSI. Most isolates exist in two phases; phase I is the motile phase and phase II the non-motile phase. Cultures that are non-motile upon primary culture may be swithched to the motile phase using a Craigie tube.
Salmonella enterica	Salmonella enterica is a rod shaped, flagellated, aerobic, Gram-negative bacterium, and a member of the genus Salmonella. S. enterica has an extraordinarily large number of serovars or strains--up to 2000 have been described. · Salmonella enterica Serovar Typhi (historically elevated to species status as S. typhi) is the disease agent in typhoid fever. The genome sequences of Serovar Typhi has been established. · Salmonella enterica Serovar Typhimurium (also known as S. typhimurium) can lead to a form of human gastroenteritis sometimes referred to as salmonellosis. · The genome sequences of serovar Typhimurium LT2 have been established. Also an analysis of the proteome of Typhimurium LT2 under differing environmental conditions has been performed .

Go to **Cram101.com** for Interactive Practice Exams for this book or virtually any of your books for $4.95/month.
And, **NEVER** highlight a book again!

Shiga toxin	Shiga toxin s are a family of related toxins with two major groups, Stx1 and Stx2, whose genes are considered to be part of the genome of lambdoid prophages. The toxins are named for Kiyoshi Shiga, who first described the bacterial origin of dysentery caused by Shigella dysenteriae. The most common sources for Shiga toxin are the bacteria S. dysenteriae and the Shigatoxigenic group of Escherichia coli (Shiga toxin EC), which includes serotype O157:H7 and other enterohemorrhagic E. coli.
Salmonellosis	Salmonellosis is an infection with Salmonella bacteria. Most persons infected with salmonella develop diarrhea, fever, vomiting, and abdominal cramps; 12 to 72 hours after infection. In most cases, the illness lasts 3 to 7 days; most affected persons recover without treatment.
Shigellosis	Shigellosis is a foodborne illness caused by infection by bacteria of the genus Shigella. Shigellosis rarely occurs in animals other than humans and other primates like monkeys and chimpanzees. The causative organism is frequently found in water polluted with human feces, and is transmitted via the fecal-oral route.
Typhoid fever	Typhoid fever Salmonella typhi or commonly just typhoid, is an illness caused by the bacterium Salmonella enterica serovar typhi. Common worldwide, it is transmitted by the ingestion of food or water contaminated with feces from an infected person. The bacteria then perforate through the intestinal wall and are phagocytosed by macrophages.
Vibrio	Vibrio is a genus of Gram-negative bacteria possessing a curved rod shape. Typically found in saltwater, Vibrio are facultative anaerobes that test positive for oxidase and do not form spores. All members of the genus are motile and have polar flagella with sheaths.
Vibrio cholerae	Vibrio cholerae is a motile gram negative curved-rod shaped bacterium with a polar flagellum that causes cholera in humans. V. cholerae and other species of the genus Vibrio belong to the gamma subdivision of the Proteobacteria. There are two major strains of V. cholerae, classic and El Tor, and numerous other serogroups.
Vibrio vulnificus	Vibrio vulnificus is a species of Gram-negative, motile, curved, rod-shaped bacteria in the genus Vibrio. Present in marine environments such as estuaries, brackish ponds, or coastal areas, V. vulnificus is closely related to V. cholerae, the causative agent of cholera.· Infection with V. vulnificus leads to rapidly expanding cellulitis or septicemia.[279] Vibrio vulnificus causes an infection often incurred after eating seafood, especially oysters; the bacteria can also enter the body through open wounds when swimming or wading in infected waters, or via puncture wounds from the spines of fish such as tilapia. Symptoms include vomiting, diarrhea, abdominal pain, and a blistering dermatitis that is sometimes mistaken for pemphigus or pemphigoid.
RecA	RecA is a 38 kilodalton Escherichia coli protein essential for the repair and maintenance of DNA. RecA has a structural and functional homolog in every species in which it has been seriously sought and serves as an archetype for this class of homologous DNA repair proteins. The homologous protein in Homo sapiens is called RAD51.

Go to **Cram101.com** for Interactive Practice Exams for this book or virtually any of your books for $4.95/month.
And, **NEVER** highlight a book again!

	RecA has multiple activities, all related to DNA repair.
Bacillus cereus	Bacillus cereus is an endemic, soil-dwelling, Gram-positive, rod-shaped, beta hemolytic bacterium. Some strains are harmful to humans and cause foodborne illness, while other strains can be beneficial as probiotics for animals. It is the cause of "Fried Rice Syndrome".
Yersinia	Yersinia is a genus of bacteria in the family Enterobacteriaceae. Yersinia are Gram-negative rod shaped bacteria, a few micrometers long and fractions of a micrometer in diameter, and are facultative anaerobes. Some members of Yersinia are pathogenic in humans.
Yersinia enterocolitica	Yersinia enterocolitica is a species of gram-negative coccobacillus-shaped bacterium, belonging to the family Enterobacteriaceae. Primarily a zoonotic disease (cattle, deer, pigs, and birds), animals that recover frequently become asymptomatic carriers of the disease. Acute Y. enterocolitica infections produce severe diarrhea in humans, along with Peyer"s patch necrosis, chronic lymphadenopathy, and hepatic or splenic abscesses.
Yersinia pestis	Yersinia pestis is a Gram-negative rod-shaped bacterium belonging to the family Enterobacteriaceae. It is a facultative anaerobe that can infect humans and other animals. Human Y. pestis infection takes three main forms: pneumonic, septicemic, and the notorious bubonic plagues.
Vibrio parahaemolyticus	Vibrio parahaemolyticus is a curved, rod-shaped, Gram-negative bacterium found in brackish saltwater, which, when ingested, causes gastrointestinal illness in humans. V. parahaemolyticus is oxidase positive, facultatively aerobic, and does not form spores. Like other members of the genus Vibrio, this species is motile, with a single, polar flagellum.
Neisseria	The Neisseria are a large family of commensal bacteria that colonize the mucosal surfaces of many animals. Of the eleven species that colonize humans, only two are pathogens. N. meningitidis and N. gonorrhoeae often cause asymptomatic infections, a commensal-like behavior.
Neisseria gonorrhoeae	Neisseria gonorrhoeae or Gonococcus, is a species of Gram-negative kidney bean-shaped diplococci bacteria responsible for the sexually transmitted disease gonorrhoea. N.gonorrhoeae was first described by Albert Neisser in 1879. Neisseria are fastidious cocci, requiring nutrient supplementation to grow in laboratory cultures.

Go to **Cram101.com** for Interactive Practice Exams for this book or virtually any of your books for $4.95/month.
And, **NEVER** highlight a book again!

Neisseria	The Neisseria are a large family of commensal bacteria that colonize the mucosal surfaces of many animals. Of the eleven species that colonize humans, only two are pathogens. N. meningitidis and N. gonorrhoeae often cause asymptomatic infections, a commensal-like behavior.
Neisseria meningitidis	Neisseria meningitidis is a heterotrophic gram-negative diplococcal bacterium best known for its role in meningitis and other forms of meningococcal disease such as meningococcemia. N. meningitidis is a major cause of morbidity and mortality in childhood in industrialized countries and is responsible for epidemics in Africa and in Asia.
	Approximately 2500 to 3500 cases of N meningitidis infection occur annually in the United States, with a case rate of about 1 in 100,000.
Staphylococcus	Staphylococcus is a genus of Gram-positive bacteria. Under the microscope they appear round , and form in grape-like clusters.
	The Staphylococcus genus include just thirty-three species.
Neisseria gonorrhoeae	Neisseria gonorrhoeae or Gonococcus, is a species of Gram-negative kidney bean-shaped diplococci bacteria responsible for the sexually transmitted disease gonorrhoea.
	N.gonorrhoeae was first described by Albert Neisser in 1879.
	Neisseria are fastidious cocci, requiring nutrient supplementation to grow in laboratory cultures.
Salmonella	Salmonella is a genus of rod-shaped, Gram-negative, non-spore forming, predominantly motile enterobacteria with diameters around 0.7 to 1.5 µm, lengths from 2 to 5 µm, and flagella which project in all directions (i.e. peritrichous.) They are chemoorganotrophs, obtaining their energy from oxidation and reduction reactions using organic sources and are facultative anaerobes; most species produce hydrogen sulfide, which can readily be detected by growing them on media containing ferrous sulfate, such as TSI. Most isolates exist in two phases; phase I is the motile phase and phase II the non-motile phase. Cultures that are non-motile upon primary culture may be swithched to the motile phase using a Craigie tube.
Salmonellosis	Salmonellosis is an infection with Salmonella bacteria. Most persons infected with salmonella develop diarrhea, fever, vomiting, and abdominal cramps; 12 to 72 hours after infection. In most cases, the illness lasts 3 to 7 days; most affected persons recover without treatment.
Syphilis	Syphilis is a sexually transmitted disease caused by the spirochetal bacterium Treponema pallidum subspecies pallidum. The route of transmission of Syphilis is almost always through sexual contact, although there are examples of congenital Syphilis via transmission from mother to child in utero.
	The signs and symptoms of Syphilis are numerous; before the advent of serological testing, precise diagnosis was very difficult.
Salt	Salt played a major role during the Civil War. Salt not only preserved food in the days before refrigeration, but was also vital in the curing of leather. Union general William Tecumseh Sherman once said that "Salt is eminently contraband", as an army that has Salt can adequately feed its men.

Go to **Cram101.com** for Interactive Practice Exams for this book or virtually any of your books for $4.95/month.
And, **NEVER** highlight a book again!

Yersinia

Yersinia is a genus of bacteria in the family Enterobacteriaceae. Yersinia are Gram-negative rod shaped bacteria, a few micrometers long and fractions of a micrometer in diameter, and are facultative anaerobes. Some members of Yersinia are pathogenic in humans.

Go to **Cram101.com** for Interactive Practice Exams for this book or virtually any of your books for $4.95/month.
And, **NEVER** highlight a book again!

Thermus aquaticus	Thermus aquaticus is a species of bacterium that can tolerate high temperatures, one of several thermophilic bacteria that belong to the Deinococcus-Thermus group. It is the source of the heat-resistant enzyme Taq DNA Polymerase, one of the most important enzymes in molecular biology because of its use in the polymerase chain reaction (PCR) DNA amplification technique.
	When studies of biological organisms in hot springs began in the 1960s, scientists thought that the life of thermophilic bacteria could not be sustained in temperatures above about 55° Celsius (131° Fahrenheit.)
Veillonella	Veillonella are gram-negative anaerobic cocci. This bacterium is well known for its lactate fermenting abilities. They are a normal bacterium in the intestines and oral mucosa of mammals.
Thermophile	A Thermophile is an organism -- a type of extremophile -- that thrives at relatively high temperatures, between 45 and 80 °C (113 and 176 °F.) Many Thermophile s are archaea.
	Thermophile s are found in various geothermally heated regions of the Earth such as hot springs like those in Yellowstone National Park and deep sea hydrothermal vents, as well as decaying plant matter such as peat bogs and compost.
Pseudomonas	Pseudomonas is a genus of gamma proteobacteria, belonging to the larger family of pseudomonads. Recently, 16S rRNA sequence analysis has redefined the taxonomy of many bacterial species. As a result the genus Pseudomonas includes strains formerly classified in the genera Chryseomonas and Flavimonas.
Nitrifying bacteria	Nitrifying bacteria are chemoautotrophic bacteria that grow by consuming inorganic nitrogen compounds. Many species of Nitrifying bacteria have complex internal membrane systems that are the location for key enzymes in nitrification: ammonia monooxygenase which oxidizes ammonia to hydroxylamine, and nitrite oxidoreductase, which oxidizes nitrite to nitrate.
	Nitrifying bacteria are widespread in soil and water, and are found in highest numbers where considerable amounts of ammonia are present (areas with extensive protein decomposition, and sewage treatment plants.)
Rhizobium	Rhizobium is a genus of Gram-negative soil bacteria that fix nitrogen. Rhizobium forms an endosymbiotic nitrogen fixing association with roots of legumes. The bacteria colonize plant cells within root nodules.
Plague	Plague is a deadly infectious disease caused by the enterobacteria Yersinia pestis (Pasteurella pestis.) Plague is a zoonotic, primarily carried by rodents (most notably rats) and spread to humans via fleas. Plague is notorious throughout history, due to the unprecedented scale of death and devastation it brought.
Prochlorococcus	Prochlorococcus is a genus of very small (0.6 µm) marine cyanobacteria with an unusual pigmentation (chlorophyll b) belonging to photosynthetic picoplankton. It is probably the most abundant photosynthetic organism on Earth.

Go to **Cram101.com** for Interactive Practice Exams for this book or virtually any of your books for $4.95/month.
And, **NEVER** highlight a book again!

	Although there had been several earlier records of very small chlorophyll-b-containing cyanobacteria in the ocean, Prochlorococcus was actually discovered in 1986 by Sallie W. (Penny) Chisholm of the Massachusetts Institute of Technology, Robert J. Olson of the Woods Hole Oceanographic Institution, and other collaborators in the Sargasso Sea using flow cytometry.
Salt	Salt played a major role during the Civil War. Salt not only preserved food in the days before refrigeration, but was also vital in the curing of leather. Union general William Tecumseh Sherman once said that "Salt is eminently contraband", as an army that has Salt can adequately feed its men.
Neisseria	The Neisseria are a large family of commensal bacteria that colonize the mucosal surfaces of many animals. Of the eleven species that colonize humans, only two are pathogens. N. meningitidis and N. gonorrhoeae often cause asymptomatic infections, a commensal-like behavior.
Neisseria meningitidis	Neisseria meningitidis is a heterotrophic gram-negative diplococcal bacterium best known for its role in meningitis and other forms of meningococcal disease such as meningococcemia. N. meningitidis is a major cause of morbidity and mortality in childhood in industrialized countries and is responsible for epidemics in Africa and in Asia. Approximately 2500 to 3500 cases of N meningitidis infection occur annually in the United States, with a case rate of about 1 in 100,000.
Typhoid fever	Typhoid fever Salmonella typhi or commonly just typhoid, is an illness caused by the bacterium Salmonella enterica serovar typhi. Common worldwide, it is transmitted by the ingestion of food or water contaminated with feces from an infected person. The bacteria then perforate through the intestinal wall and are phagocytosed by macrophages.
Prevotella	Prevotella is a genus of bacteria. "Bacteroides melaninogenicus" has recently been reclassified and split into Prevotella melaninogenica and Prevotella intermedia. Several species have been implicated in oral disease.
Staphylococcus	Staphylococcus is a genus of Gram-positive bacteria. Under the microscope they appear round , and form in grape-like clusters. The Staphylococcus genus include just thirty-three species.
Staphylococcus aureus	Staphylococcus aureus is the most common cause of staph infections. It is a spherical bacterium, frequently part of the skin flora found in the nose and on skin. About 20% of the population are long-term carriers of S. aureus.

Go to **Cram101.com** for Interactive Practice Exams for this book or virtually any of your books for $4.95/month.
And, **NEVER** highlight a book again!

Neisseria	The Neisseria are a large family of commensal bacteria that colonize the mucosal surfaces of many animals. Of the eleven species that colonize humans, only two are pathogens. N. meningitidis and N. gonorrhoeae often cause asymptomatic infections, a commensal-like behavior.
Neisseria gonorrhoeae	Neisseria gonorrhoeae or Gonococcus, is a species of Gram-negative kidney bean-shaped diplococci bacteria responsible for the sexually transmitted disease gonorrhoea. N.gonorrhoeae was first described by Albert Neisser in 1879. Neisseria are fastidious cocci, requiring nutrient supplementation to grow in laboratory cultures.
Salmonella	Salmonella is a genus of rod-shaped, Gram-negative, non-spore forming, predominantly motile enterobacteria with diameters around 0.7 to 1.5 µm, lengths from 2 to 5 µm, and flagella which project in all directions (i.e. peritrichous.) They are chemoorganotrophs, obtaining their energy from oxidation and reduction reactions using organic sources and are facultative anaerobes; most species produce hydrogen sulfide, which can readily be detected by growing them on media containing ferrous sulfate, such as TSI. Most isolates exist in two phases; phase I is the motile phase and phase II the non-motile phase. Cultures that are non-motile upon primary culture may be swithched to the motile phase using a Craigie tube.
Bacillus cereus	Bacillus cereus is an endemic, soil-dwelling, Gram-positive, rod-shaped, beta hemolytic bacterium. Some strains are harmful to humans and cause foodborne illness, while other strains can be beneficial as probiotics for animals. It is the cause of "Fried Rice Syndrome".
Bacillus stearothermophilus	Bacillus stearothermophilus (or GeoBacillus stearothermophilus) is a rod-shaped, Gram-positive bacterium and a member of the division Firmicutes. The bacteria is a thermophile and is widely distributed in soil, hot springs, ocean sediment, and is a cause of spoilage in food products. It will grow within a temperature range of 30-75 degrees celsius.
Yersinia	Yersinia is a genus of bacteria in the family Enterobacteriaceae. Yersinia are Gram-negative rod shaped bacteria, a few micrometers long and fractions of a micrometer in diameter, and are facultative anaerobes. Some members of Yersinia are pathogenic in humans.
Yersinia pestis	Yersinia pestis is a Gram-negative rod-shaped bacterium belonging to the family Enterobacteriaceae. It is a facultative anaerobe that can infect humans and other animals. Human Y. pestis infection takes three main forms: pneumonic, septicemic, and the notorious bubonic plagues.
Saccharomyces	Saccharomyces is a genus in the kingdom of fungi that includes many species of yeast. Saccharomyces is from Latin meaning sugar fungi. Many members of this genus are considered very important in food production.
Saccharomyces cerevisiae	Saccharomyces cerevisiae is a species of budding yeast. It is perhaps the most useful yeast owing to its use since ancient times in baking and brewing. It is believed that it was originally isolated from the skins of grapes
Pseudomonas	Pseudomonas is a genus of gamma proteobacteria, belonging to the larger family of pseudomonads.

Go to **Cram101.com** for Interactive Practice Exams for this book or virtually any of your books for $4.95/month.
And, **NEVER** highlight a book again!

	Recently, 16S rRNA sequence analysis has redefined the taxonomy of many bacterial species. As a result the genus Pseudomonas includes strains formerly classified in the genera Chryseomonas and Flavimonas.
RecA	RecA is a 38 kilodalton Escherichia coli protein essential for the repair and maintenance of DNA. RecA has a structural and functional homolog in every species in which it has been seriously sought and serves as an archetype for this class of homologous DNA repair proteins. The homologous protein in Homo sapiens is called RAD51. RecA has multiple activities, all related to DNA repair.
Rhizobium	Rhizobium is a genus of Gram-negative soil bacteria that fix nitrogen. Rhizobium forms an endosymbiotic nitrogen fixing association with roots of legumes. The bacteria colonize plant cells within root nodules.
Vibrio	Vibrio is a genus of Gram-negative bacteria possessing a curved rod shape. Typically found in saltwater, Vibrio are facultative anaerobes that test positive for oxidase and do not form spores. All members of the genus are motile and have polar flagella with sheaths.
Vibrio fischeri	Vibrio fischeri is a gram-negative rod-shaped bacterium found globally in the marine environments. V. fischeri has bioluminescent properties, and is found predominantly in symbiosis with various marine animals, such as the bobtail squid. It is heterotrophic and moves by means of flagella.

Go to **Cram101.com** for Interactive Practice Exams for this book or virtually any of your books for $4.95/month.
And, **NEVER** highlight a book again!

CPSIA information can be obtained at www.ICGtesting.com
Printed in the USA
268546BV00001B/223/P

9 781616 542665